A Mountain View

A Mountain View

A Memoir of Childhood Summers
on Upper Saranac Lake

Lewis Spence

 Syracuse University Press

Copyright © 2002 by Syracuse University Press
Syracuse, New York 13244-5160
All Rights Reserved

First Edition 2002
02 03 04 05 06 07   6 5 4 3 2 1

The paper used in this publication meets the minimum requirements
of American National Standard for Information Sciences—Permanence
of Paper for Printed Library Materials, ANSI Z39.48–1984.∞™

Library of Congress Cataloging-in-Publication Data

Spence, Lewis, 1920–1998.
   A mountain view : a memoir of childhood summers on Upper Saranac Lake / Lewis
Spence.—1st ed.
    p. cm.
   ISBN 0-8156-0728-8 (cl. : alk. paper)
   1. Spence, Lewis, 1920–1998-Childhood and youth. 2. Upper Saranac Lake Region
(N.Y.)—Social life and customs—20th century. 3. Upper Saranac Lake Region
(N.Y.)—Biography. 4. Adirondack Mountains Region (N.Y.)—Social life and
customs—20th century. 5. Adirondack Mountains Region (N.Y.)—Biography. I. Title.
F127.F8 S64 2001
974.7'55—dc21   2001043385

Manufactured in the United States of America

CONTENTS

ILLUSTRATIONS

LEWIS SPENCE was born in New York City on Halloween, 1920. Upon graduation from Harvard, he served with the Coast Guard in the Arctic during World War II. After the war, he worked as a reporter for the *Schenectady Union Star* in upstate New York. He later worked for *Time* magazine and the Ford Foundation.

In 1953, Spence founded Lewis Spence & Co., a consulting firm that specialized in teaching business writing at corporations. He was an avid gardener.

Until his death in 1998, Spence and his wife Ellie, a librarian, lived in Cranbury, N.J. and summered on Saranac Lake. He is survived by his wife, three sons, a daughter, and eight grandchildren.

PREFACE

SEVERAL WEEKS after my grandfather, Lewis Spence, died at his home in Cranbury, N.J., Syracuse University Press accepted the manuscript of *A Mountain View* for publication. Lewis was seventy-seven and had spent the last decade of his life writing this memoir of boyhood summers at his grandfather's camp on Upper Saranac Lake in the Adirondacks.

Those summers, warmly described in *A Mountain View*, forged my grandfather's connection to the Adirondacks, instilling in him a devotion to the unexplored swamps, deep forests, and clear lakes of that mountain region. As his grandfather's favorite, Lewis spent the summers of 1931 to 1934 alone with the crotchety old man at Wood-wil, the Adirondack estate that my great-great-grandfather built in the mid-1920s. Under the questionable guidance of Oscar, the camp's Swedish handyman, the young Lewis was free to explore a seven-mile-long lake full of hidden bays and rocky ledges. There he learned to hunt, sail, and fish, an adventurer with few visitors for company. It seems a lonely life for a young boy, yet these summers on Upper Saranac formed my grandfather's most cherished memories.

In the 1950s Woodwil was sold to a family that could better afford its upkeep. It was Lewis's good fortune that forty acres were left to be divided between him and his cousin, John R. Dunlap IV. In time, both families built their own modest camps on Markham Point, half a mile across the peninsula from Woodwil.

When my grandfather started taking his young family to the Adirondacks, the world was a different place than it was when his grandfather first settled on Upper Saranac Lake. The Adirondacks were no longer the fashionable playground of America's elite. Lewis's grandfather, John Robertson Dunlap, was part of a privileged class that firmly believed in its own superiority. My great-great-grandfather hated blacks, Jews, Italians, and all other non-Anglo-Saxons, believing them, from what he considered a scientific standpoint, to be inferior. It was a point of view he shared with many of his social set. Although Lewis came to resemble his grandfather in many ways, he vehemently rejected Dunlap's xenophobia.

Lewis raised his own children to reject bigotry. In fact, two of them married Jews—his daughter Olivia and his second son, Harry, my father. Reading Lewis's memoir, I am amused to think how horrified the old man would be to learn that some of his great-great-grandchildren were descendants of Jews who have lived for five hundred years on the land that is now Israel.

Beyond merely rejecting his own grandfather's narrow values, my grandfather actively worked to further racial and economic equality. He was an early supporter of civil rights, and in the 1960s he tried, albeit unsuccessfully, to start a school in New Jersey for young African American boys.

The Spence family camp was considerably more modest than Woodwil, but my cousins and I spent part of every summer on the lake, repeating our grandfather's experiences. Like him, we set forth in boats, learned to swim and sail in the lake's clear waters, camped on the same islands, and climbed the same rocks.

But, to be honest, Lewis Spence was not a patient grandfather. He didn't like having small children around. When our families did visit, he was preoccupied with his own camp improvement projects. I remember walking toward the house when I was seven, crying, only to be stopped by my grandfather, who bellowed, "This is not a place for children to cry!" He forbade me from entering the house.

Nevertheless, through all those years of visiting the Adirondacks, my cousins and I learned the same devotion to the land that my grandfather had learned from his grandfather. As a child, I eagerly anticipated the five-hour drive from Boston to Saranac Lake, where we would spend two weeks every summer. Nothing was more thrilling than the first swim of the season or an evening ride in the motorboat with my father.

My grandfather mellowed with the years and seemed genuinely glad to see our growing clan gather for annual reunions at the lake. Then, in 1995, a family tragedy helped to bring us all closer. My twenty-six-year-old cousin Colin, a paramedic, was killed when his ambulance was involved in a traffic accident. We scattered a portion of Colin's ashes on Saranac Lake and committed to gathering in the Adirondacks every year on Labor Day.

Three years later, when my grandfather died, we gathered to sprinkle his ashes on the lake and to place a stone next to Colin's outside the rustic Church of the Ascension near the site of the old Saranac Inn.

During those last years of his life, as cancer slowly consumed his body, Lewis continued to work on his Saranac camp as he had always done, replacing rotting beams on the deck and clearing trees to maintain the lake view.

My grandfather did not take us fishing, teach us to sail, or hike with us up mountain trails. But as I stood on our dock in the middle of the night last summer, looking up at the Adirondack sky filled with stars and listening to the sound of wind in the tall pines, I realized the importance of the legacy he left for us all.

REBECCA SPENCE

ACKNOWLEDGMENTS

THE SPENCE FAMILY thanks Ann Hochschild Poole, whose enthusiasm for this book contributed to its publication and helped ease Lewis's last days. They are also grateful to Julie Michaels for her editing skills and to Chris Jerome for her accuracy as a copy editor and her keen knowledge of Adirondack history. Thanks also to Janet Decker, head of the local history section of the Saranac Lake Public Library, for providing the photos of Woodwil.

A Mountain View

 CHAPTER ONE

FROM THE TIME I WAS ELEVEN through my fourteenth birthday it was variously my good fortune, delight, loneliness, and sorrow to spend a large part of my summers as the sole companion of my grandfather, John Dunlap, at his camp on Upper Saranac Lake, in the northern tier of the Adirondack Mountains. John Robertson Dunlap, lately of Lexington, Kentucky, was then well into his seventies. He had begun building the camp in 1926, at the height of the stock market boom, to serve as his summer residence. Having financed it with proceeds from the sale of his business, he completed it two years later, just in time for the crash of 1929 to all but wipe him out. With this disaster, followed by the death of his second wife a year later, it devolved on me, for reasons still mysterious, to be his favorite grandchild and anointed companion for those sad but golden years of the early 1930s.

To understand what is meant by an Adirondack *camp*, one must go back to the turn of the century and a decade earlier, when the extravagant vulgarity of America's Gilded Age capitalism had given way to what rich men liked to think was a more cultivated indulgence in conspicuous consumption. Instead of erecting marble palaces (quaintly called *cottages*) in Newport, Rhode Island, a number of the more discriminating rich turned to the simpler joys of rustic life. They built themselves not camps, to be sure, but miniature

3

villages on the shores of several of the wilder and more beautiful Adirondack lakes. Mind you, these villages were not inhabited collectively by a congenial covey of rich men. Instead, each rich man built his own small village, which besides the main lodge and dining hall, consisted of its own power plant, water tower, and icehouse. There were also sufficient boathouses, guide houses, servants' quarters, guest houses, and other sundry outbuildings to accommodate a modest house party of twenty to twenty-five friends and relatives, in addition to a sturdy force of servants and attendants.

Besides their spacious opulence, another distinctive feature of these camps—commonly known today as Great Camps—was their determined and self-conscious emphasis on rusticity. The prevailing mode of architecture was what can best be described as "Adirondack rustic." Most featured a proliferation of wide verandahs, fieldstone chimneys, fake log siding, dark-stained timbers, and shingled roofs reminiscent of Swiss chalets, but they were distinctly American in size, comfort, and interior appointments. And, of course, staring out above every fireplace, adorning every bedroom, draping over banisters, and menacing the dining room table were menageries of stuffed moose and deer heads, antlers, animal hides, and mounted birds and fishes. (Some iconoclasts, such as cereal heiress Marjorie Merriweather Post, went in for leopard skins, water buffalo heads, crocodile hides, and the remains of other creatures certainly not native to the Adirondacks.) Usually only in the kitchen and bathroom could one escape this grotesque collection of the prizes of venery.

Amid these surroundings, wealthy Americans could savor in comfort the pleasures of wilderness living, disporting themselves as latter-day Natty Bumppos, complete with .30–.30 rifles and fishing poles, canoes and guideboats—with the latter being unique Adirondack crafts, designed to be rowed, not paddled.

The site of Grandfather's camp, Upper Saranac, one of the largest lakes in the region, had more than its share of these splendid habitations. Reflecting the common but peculiar mores of the era, they were situated in a remarkable manner; that is, the wealthy Jewish families—the Baches, Lewisohns, Kahns, and Seligmans—inhabited the southern end of the lake. Beyond the Narrows, the gentile rich—the Bedfords, Earls, Du Ponts, Rockefellers—peopled the northern end of the lake. And never the twain would meet, believe you me.

This division of the lake into two separate realms had no immediate impact on me as a child, but as I tell later, it suited Grandfather, with his troglodytic views on race and religion—views benightedly shared, I should add, almost universally by his social contemporaries. On one hand he wanted to keep as wide a gulf as the Grand Canyon between himself and the rich Jewish "campers," but at the same time he took pride in showing the magnificent camps of those same Jews to his guests on boat tours of the lake.

Today those homes, Jewish as well as gentile, have almost all been converted into summer camps for children, divided up into second homes, or turned into inns or lodges donated—at a pleasant tax savings—to universities such as Colgate and St. Lawrence to be used as alumni playgrounds. The huge Lewisohn camp, for example, with its forty-odd buildings, now ironically houses the Young Life camp, a quasi-religious organization, Christian by creed, that runs programs for children throughout the East and Midwest. What was once the William Rockefeller camp is today the Point, by its own boast the toniest hostelry in the land, nicking its patrons, at last report, an average of one thousand dollars per couple per night.

But to return to Grandfather, his camp contained seven separate buildings housing eight double bedrooms, plus servants' quarters, a water tower, and a network of painstakingly constructed wooden walkways interconnecting the little village. To make up in style what the camp might lack in size, Grandfather brought the forest right into the living room of the main lodge with huge log trusses for the two-story roof and, at each end of the fifty-foot room, twin staircases fashioned of split-pine timbers with the bark carefully tacked on. The mantel was fashioned from a mammoth birch log, its white bark blackened by seasons of smoke and heat. Outside, the main lodge was clad with slabs of timber cleverly disguised to look like genuine log cabin construction. The broad roofs of both the verandah and boathouse were sheathed in birch bark to give them the appearance of the Indian longhouse, where the braves of tribe met in solemn council.

But this artfully contrived rusticity, Grandfather's greatest pride, had its price: despite all the advice, concoctions, and sprays of state forestry experts, the wood bugs invaded. They got into the magnificent spruce trusses and split-pine stair treads, so that summer evenings over cribbage or dominoes were punctuated by the grinding crunch of insects munching away under the bark. There was no danger, so Grandfather was assured, of the buildings one day collapsing in a spectacular, powdery *whoomph* of sawdust. But each spring when we arrived, Oscar, Grandfather's "guide," spent hours retacking the bark. Of course the grinding of the wood bugs' mandibles was an unpleasant counterpoint to Grandfather's grandiloquent explication of authentic Adirondack architecture.

To offset to some degree the gloom of all this faux rusticity, the main lodge, in particular the living room, was furnished with summery furniture. Two large wicker sofas angled to take in the view of the lake through the large picture window at the front of the room. On each side of the massive fieldstone fireplace were two wicker fan chairs that looked to my young eyes like the perfect seat for Sax Rohmer's sinister Dr. Fu Manchu, with his long, stringy mustache and talonlike fingernails. And of course on almost every available square foot of wall space were the ritually mounted deer and moose heads. Of these, one had been shot by Grandfather's second son, Jack, at enormous expense on a Canadian hunting expedition; the other had been bought at auction by Mother for some ten dollars. There were also stuffed fish and birds of prey, plus the indispensable bearskin rug, complete with head and exposed fangs, on the floor before the hearth. As was the custom, Grandfather had bought most of these splendid trophies at the run-down secondhand shops that still populate towns throughout the Adirondacks.

By the French doors that gave out onto the verandah at each end of the living room were two small built-in bookcases, one of which was filled with volumes of a biography of Thomas Jefferson that Grandfather had written years earlier. As a child I thought these books were all part of a multivolume work that Grandfather had spent decades researching and writing, only to learn later that they were but remaindered copies of the same one-volume, self-published edition.

Plumbing and electricity for Grandfather's compound were provided, respectively, by water pumped from the lake (potable in those days) to the water tower and by a Delco plant housed in a small building to the rear of the main lodge. The electricity was stored in banks of heavy glass batteries that had to be recharged by a gasoline-powered generator each morning. Grandfather was forever worried lest the batteries be drained to a point beyond recharging, so in the evening we regularly sat in semidarkness until he granted permission to light a lamp or two. Such newfangled gadgets as a radio and a refrigerator were forbidden. Grandfather got his news from the newspaper, and the icebox was stocked with blocks cut during the winter and stored in mountains of sawdust in the icehouse.

One marvel of twentieth-century technology he did permit was a telephone, located in the pantry off the kitchen. It was housed in a wooden box mounted on the wall and had a projecting mouthpiece. On one side was a small crank that roused the operator, and on the other was the receiver, attached by a short cable, which hung in a U-shaped hook. That telephone was used almost exclusively by our cook, Julia, to order groceries from the market in the town of Saranac

Lake. As for Grandfather, I don't believe he ever really understood the function of a telephone. Whenever he used it, he bellowed so into the mouthpiece that he might just as well have stood on the verandah and shouted to whomever he wished to address. The rare long-distance calls, from my mother at home on Long Island or from one of Grandfather's acquaintances, were regarded in much the same light as the communications between astronauts and Mission Control in Houston. Calling times were set in an exchange of letters, and the recipient of the communication would be posted in the pantry a full fifteen minutes before the appointed time. All these preparations were in a way superfluous, however, for such were the burblings and squeaks generated by the underwater cable that it was lucky if one could catch every tenth word the person at the other end of the line uttered. But never mind: through the telephone we were clued in to the world at large and to the dawning glow of the "information age."

The camp was located at the end of a long, narrow peninsula at the northern, "gentile" end of the lake and thus commanded an incomparable view that was without question its most stunning attribute. That view compensated, in the soft beauty of forest and mountain, water and sky, for what Grandfather could not create with hard cash. To the west, the broad verandah of the main lodge, perched high on a rock ledge, looked directly through the Narrows a full five miles down the lake to the low, dark humps of Panther and Stony Creek Mountains. To the southeast lay the panorama of Ampersand, Saddleback, Sawtooth, and, far in the blue distance, hunched over the shoulder of nearby Boot Bay Mountain like a scowling thunderhead, Mount Marcy, highest in the Adirondacks at more than five thousand feet.

Grandfather's property consisted of some fifty acres, all in forest, spanning the full width of the peninsula. This position delighted him because it meant he owned nearly a mile of enviable lakefront. After the stock market crash, he envisioned recouping his fortune by selling off building lots to bankrupt gentlemen like himself. Also, his fifty acres were ringed by thousands of acres owned by the State of New York, vast tracts of it the impenetrable Black Pond Swamp, which the state constitution had deeded "forever wild" to the citizens of New York. This protected Grandfather in his mountain fastness from the *lily pickers,* his favorite term for the riffraff who in his view had already overrun Lake George and whose advent he regarded with the fury of a Roman centurion facing the Visigoths.

Grandfather looked on this modest—by Adirondack standards—domain as the natural prerogative and heritage of his landowning Kentucky forebears. As a victim of southern mythology, Grandfather believed that ownership of land was the all but divine benediction on God's anointed overlord, the Scotch-Irish, Anglo-Saxon gentleman. Even in the darkest days of the Great Depression, when many of the camps on the lake were closed, Grandfather employed throughout the summer a crew of four or five men to hew and saw his fifty acres into a woodland park. Similarly, Oscar and Julia, a Swedish couple, were there to cook for and tend to us, as befit our station. In the boathouse were lodged the essential Chris-Craft, an outboard, canoes, and guideboats, and, to me most splendid of all, a large tin workboat powered by a monstrous cast-iron one-cylinder engine that had the kick of a buffalo. Once started, this craft set up such a deafening, thumping vibration that it made the water in the bilge leap and dance six inches over the floorboards and the sound reverberate off every point and bay within a mile radius. All of this, of course, was paid for by continual inroads on Grandfather's small remaining capital and held up, as I have said, by the insanely optimistic hope of selling off the choicer lakefront sites to other retired southern gentlemen.

As a final, climactic gesture, Grandfather named the camp Woodwil, an abbreviation of the name Woodrow Wilson. Actually, Thomas Jefferson, about whom Grandfather had written that unreadable biography, was his greatest hero, but nothing very rustic sounding could be made of his name. Furthermore, Grandfather had known Wilson slightly. He also admired him, and, perhaps most important of all, Wilson was a southern gentleman. This practice of naming places and things with strange inversions and anagrams of people's names or objects was, I think, endemic to Grandfather's generation. Thus, the Chris-Craft was named *Arodasi,* which I learned only years later was my stepgrandmother's name spelled backward.

Here at Woodwil, this glorious but outlandishly pretentious place, Grandfather, Julia, Oscar, and I lived for those four long summers. We were much alone. For the first two years the camp could be reached only by boat. Then, in 1932, as a further enticement to buyers, Grandfather added a private four-mile-long road through the wilderness. It did little good. After the 1929 crash, the Adirondacks suffered a woeful decline as a fashionable summer resort. During those years the region offered little in the way of social life for the eccentric pairing of a seventy-five-year-old man and a twelve-year-old boy. Yet in this solitariness, isolated by thousands of acres of primeval forest and swamp and a seven-mile-long lake full of hidden bays, broad stretches of open water, and a shoreline of twenty-foot rock cliffs and white sand beaches overarched by wind-toppled pines, I first learned the cruel joys of independence and solitude.

SUMMER AT THE CAMP began in late May and lasted through Labor Day. We arrived with the last frosts of the old winter, when the pale green spring foliage of maple, beech, and birch was bright against the dark evergreen of the pine, hemlock, and spruce forest. In those three months, interrupted by occasional visits from my mother and a few guests, usually school chums whom my mother selected and sent up to keep me company, the four of us—Grandfather, Oscar, Julia, and I—lived an existence almost primitive in its daily routine, yet sophisticated in its human relationships and division of labor. In good capitalistic fashion Grandfather gave the orders, Julia and Oscar obeyed, and I observed.

Every day I watched Oscar dig the ice from under the sawdust in the icehouse, charge the banks of batteries in the powerhouse, haul the coal for Julia's kitchen stove, fetch the mail, polish the Chris-Craft, sweep the walkways, mix the fuel for the outboard, and perform countless other chores. When I look back on it, I don't know how Oscar was able to stand my watching, let alone the work. The only privacy he had was in bed and in the bathroom. (Every time he peed in the woods, I had to take mine out and prove I could squirt even farther than he.) There was hardly a moment in the day when he didn't have my eyes fixed on him, my footsteps at his heels, and my questions to cheer the monotonous forest.

Perhaps it was the stolidness of his Swedish character that allowed Oscar to endure me. To tell the truth, however, he wasn't like most Swedes. Oscar was short, dark, bandy-legged, devious, untruthful, and servile. He was always filthy; he shaved only about every third day, chewed tobacco, picked his nose, and swore. But I loved him dearly. In his youth a muzzle-loading rifle had exploded in his face, and he regularly let me feel the shattered cheekbones that slid about under his skin. It was the sort of physical disability that children, with their savage little natures, love to know about. I was delighted with his audacity when he disobeyed Grandfather, pocketed the change he got back on the groceries, or lied to Julia about the time he wasted while marketing. I knew no one else who could belch or fart whenever he wanted. Stopping in the middle of a wooden walk, he would lift a leg and let fly with a superb, robust fart that made him roll his eyes and sigh with pleasure. Then he would whistle and snort, hold his nose, and wave his hand to fan away the smell, cursing beautifully.

"Jesus Christ, Bud, did you ever smell anything that stank so?"

he'd ask. "Goddamn, I must be rotting inside." (*Bud* was the regular-fella, masculine-sounding nickname Grandfather had bestowed on me. He thought the name I'd been given by my immediate family—Bubs—was woefully effete and sissy sounding, just too much eastern frippery for the favorite grandson of a Kentucky gentleman.)

Grandfather heartily detested Oscar, or at least only tolerated him with a sneering condescension. Periodically, after he had caught Oscar in some contemptible peccadillo, he would mutter threats that he was going to get rid of him or have him horsewhipped. However, Julia was an excellent cook and a splendid woman; also, Oscar's thieving servility perfectly fitted Grandfather's pretensions.

Grandfather really was from Kentucky, and he really was called Colonel Dunlap, although he had never been near the army. But the title sat on him quite naturally, so what did it matter whether it was real or fake? He had the bearing of a colonel. Let me emphasize, there was no stereotypical handlebar mustache and goatee, no flowing white hair and wide-brimmed hat, no iced mint julep always at hand. Still, he had some of the expected physical attributes. He was spare and tall, six feet two, and he did sport a moustache, but it was a small bristly one. His hair was chalk white, but he wore it clipped short, and most of it was a toupee, tailor-made from tresses of his wife's hair. He was noticeably lame, not from a duel or a Kentucky vendetta, but from a youthful infection in his hip that froze the socket and left one leg an inch or so shorter than the other. This disability entitled him to the elegance of a cane, and when he stood, his weight on the good leg and the cane set at a rakish angle, he had a properly patrician look. He had a narrow, high forehead, heavily hooded eyes, and a prominent, fleshy nose, slightly hooked.

To the best of my recollection, Grandfather wore a three-piece suit almost every day of his life. Occasionally he would make a concession to comfort or heat and unbutton his vest while we played dominoes or cribbage of an evening. He was never without a hat outdoors. I remember the heavy gold watch chain he wore across his slight paunch. It was attached to a Seth Thomas watch that he claimed, with his usual hyperbole, was the finest timekeeping instrument made. He always wore a pearl stickpin in his tie, and a pince-nez on a black ribbon rested in his breast pocket.

Despite his personal appearance and mien, Grandfather had the temperament and outlook of a battle-worn general. A man with few friends, he was often irritable. Most of his cronies were dead; of those who remained he was sharply critical. He insisted on the formalities of good manners: the firm handshake with gentlemen, the slight bow and tipped hat to ladies, and strict decorum at the dining table. In a word, he demanded order, promptness, and the eye-to-eye contact of one honorable man with another.

Nevertheless, a sly humor lurked beneath his crust of conventional reserve, along with a playfulness that showed itself in amused tolerance of my boyish awkwardness and naïveté. In his old age he had a strong but contemptuous regard for politics and thought, naturally, that the contemporary batch of political leaders were a poor lot compared to those of his younger years. His consuming passion, however, was genealogy, and he was forever writing to towns and parishes in England, Scotland, and Northern Ireland for birth, baptism, and burial records of anyone bearing a name connected with his own or that of his first wife (because she was the only one to bear him children). Accompanying this obsession was an unabashed snobbery encompassing racial and religious views that would singe the soul of any right-thinking, humane person today. Simply put, Grandfather was anti all the races, nationalities, and creeds of the world except the Protestant Anglo-Saxons and Celts of the British Isles.

This bigotry left a rather small circle for Grandfather to acknowledge as civilized beings, but he graciously made exceptions for any Jews, French, Italians, or what-you-will who had enough instinct for flattery to call him Colonel Dunlap and yield him first place in all personal matters. Such fellows immediately experienced what amounted to a total blood transfusion that rendered them as fair-skinned, blue-eyed, and sandy-haired as Lord Melbourne himself. As evidence of this burning conviction of our superiority, Grandfather was wont to seize my hand and trace with his forefinger the faint blue web of veins at my wrist, pronouncing in sibylline tones: "Don't you ever forget it, young man, that's blue blood that flows in those veins, the finest, purest blood that God ever gave to man. There's a host of ancestors who expect you to live up to the high standards they set." Of course, Grandfather was too much the patriot and Jeffersonian Democrat to embrace the froufrou of titles and coats of arms. In the family genealogy, another unreadable book he wrote, he traced the Dunlap clan back more than a thousand years to the early Scots. The name meant "bend in the stream" in ancient Gaelic. His ancestors had all been of stalwart, good yeoman stock—farmers, cattlemen, printers. (He even claimed kinship with the Dunlap who printed the Declaration of Independence.) With such a lineage there was no room for a class system or for any ordering of society that placed one man above another. Grandfather, in one of those contradictions to which we are all heir, was a sworn egalitarian: every man and woman as good as he—so long as they didn't get too close.

As a child I drank in all this muddled moonshine with the unthinking acceptance of a goldfish. I was more interested in what Grandfather gave me, not what he told me. When not trailing after Oscar, I was Grandfather's errand boy, boatman, and orderly, all of which services were paid for at rates ranging from a penny to a dime. It was my job to take him around to the other side of his peninsula in the outboard to inspect the makeshift docks and steps he was having built on those mythically valuable building lots. I was also detailed to escort him on tours of the birch-lined walks through his woodland park, to fetch his glasses, or to bring him the local newspaper. For each of these errands, a cascade of copper and silver passed between us.

But Grandfather was not a Scot and had not been a successful businessman for nothing. Each evening, at either dominoes or cribbage, the stack of my day's earnings drained away coin by coin to his side of the table—even though he would often give me a handicap of ten, twenty, twenty-five points, let me retake turns on which I had obviously made a stupid mistake, or even hint to me the strengths and weaknesses of his own hand. Watching my treasure disappear, I never cried or sulked and refused to go on. Grandfather's humor and playfulness always saved the day.

"Come on, now, Bud, you're smart enough to beat this old dodo," he'd tell me. "You've just had a run of bad luck. Tell you what. For every game you win, I'll double the bets. How's that?" And sure enough, he'd let me win just frequently enough to amass winnings that would eventually land in his own pocket.

Beyond bribery, however, Grandfather won my affections by dubbing me at age ten the crown prince of the family. In my mother and father's generation the Dunlaps had turned discouragingly barren. Out of seven potential breeders, this group had produced only four offspring—my elder brother, myself, a just-born younger sister, and a cousin who was Grandfather's namesake and the son of an uncle with whom Grandfather was barely on speaking terms. Within this group I had little competition. Grandfather dismissed the other members of my generation with a frostiness close to dry ice.

Chief among my positive attributes was my love for the Adirondacks, which alone seemed enough to win Grandfather's heart. Not that I was much of a hunter or cared a great deal for flora and fauna. To me a fly rod was as sporting an instrument as a knitting needle and just as likely to end up snarled in skeins of line. Nor did I love the animals of the forest, beyond my desire to slaughter as many as possible. I was particularly fond of red squirrels, whose skins, after crude tanning by tacking on a board and smothering in salt, I kept in a metal strongbox out in the woods behind the powerhouse. So rank was the stink of rotting hide that even Oscar begged off repeated invitations to inspect my collection.

Quite simply, it was the indulgence and freedom at Woodwil that made me love it so. Alone in youthful fantasy, I was lord of boats and canoes. The forest was my private domain, filled with paths I was sure no one had trod before. There were eagles then in the Adirondacks and osprey and great blue heron. Out on the water in the tin workboat, the thump of the engine hammering loud against the shoreline, I could follow their flight, imagining myself a Hiawatha who could speak their language and know their secret ways. In my self-centered child's mind, abetted by Grandfather's indulgence, I alone had discovered the wilderness, safely solitary and unchallenged by others my own age. At opposite ends of our life spans, Grandfather and I shared an arrogance and illusion that although different were equally pretentious and absurd. He spoiled me outrageously, but the spoiling, I have often thought, was of such a richness as to compensate for the cramps I have suffered for it since.

AND THEN THERE WAS JULIA, cook, housekeeper, sub-rosa financial manager, and, in a subtle sense, Grandfather's rein and conscience. A large-bosomed, solidly built woman, she had the round face of a Breughel peasant and the disposition of a sternly proud but secretly compassionate Puritan. Julia had worked for Grandfather off and on for more than forty years. She remembered my mother and two uncles as children and was now passing on to the third generation. She looked on me as a sort of foster grandchild, to be saved only by her discipline from becoming, under Grandfather's indulgence, a spoiled, pernicious nuisance. She and Oscar had not married until their late thirties, and way back in my memory I recall a son who, as Julia would say, came to no good.

As compensation, she had Oscar. His antic japes and occasional drunkenness gave her the essential cross to bear, just heavy enough to fuse her spine in a posture of martyrdom but not so burdensome as to humble her pride in her own virtue. She was rigorous, but could be palely tolerant of others' sins. She was argumentative and so convinced of her own rectitude that when she set her jaw in stubborn assertion of her point of view, Leif Eriksson himself would have quailed. Yet, when caught off guard or in the hilarity of utter, irremediable disaster, such as a chicken roasted to a frazzle, no one else could have pronounced the word *shit* with such gusto. Julia was Swedish dourness rendered humane through marriage to a Bert Lahr turned handyman.

Still, she was genuinely fond of Oscar, I am sure. For two full years she came and cooked for my mother in our house in suburban Long Island, leaving Oscar to do I know not what. And each winter she had no compunction about leaving him for a job in Montclair, New Jersey, or St. Petersburg, Florida. Yet the neglect, I suspect, was in a backhanded way a gesture of affection, permitting each some months of freedom from the other. Oscar was in one sense an indignity to Julia, but an indignity that reminded her of her superior fortitude and endurance.

At the other extreme, Grandfather and Julia treated each other with the same suspicious canniness that two old wolves employ to protect their separate territories. Grandfather's post was the wicker desk in front of the large plate-glass window overlooking the lake. For a good three hours each morning he spent his time hatching plans for his building ventures or composing letters to pastors in remote Scottish villages. Julia's perch was the huge coal stove in the kitchen. Although the Delco power plant could barely be induced, even with obscenities and cussing from Oscar, to light up a single bulb to the brilliance of a well-trimmed lantern, Julia was convinced that her lack of an efficient electric or gas stove was a deprivation Grandfather had imposed in his Scottish miserliness.

The coal stove was her palpable, personal enemy. If her words had been actualities, that stove would have corroded and disintegrated under a heap of offal. She struck it with heavy iron skillets, shook down the fire with vengeful fury, and so complained of the fumes and ashes that it was a wonder we all didn't perish of black lung. Several times a summer, while serving meals, she would announce with an irate imperiousness that the meat or dessert was not properly done.

"But it's not my fault. I can't do a thing with that stove," she would say, stationed threateningly beside Grandfather's chair and holding the serving spoon as menacingly as a mace to remind him with Swedish subtlety that he should not trifle with her. This challenge was a signal for Grandfather to taste the food, roll it delectably around his tongue, and then, looking up at Julia, pronounce with a roguish panache: "Capital, Julia, capital!" At which arrant hypocrisy Julia would sniff loudly and march back into the kitchen, leaving the swinging door to pump desolately back and forth.

The most dramatic confrontations between Grandfather and Julia took place across the full width of the living room, with Grandfather sitting at his desk and Julia standing feet apart, arms crossed over her bosom in a posture of defiant insurrection.

Julia: "Mr. Dunlap, I've no coal in my kitchen for the stove."

Grandfather, turning ever so slowly in his chair to peer at her over his pince-nez: "So! And why not, for heaven's sake?"

Julia: "Oscar hasn't brought it."

Grandfather, impatiently: "Well, tell him to, Julia, tell him to."

Julia: "I have. He says there is none."

Grandfather, incredulous: "None? Come, Julia, you must be exaggerating. There must be some."

Julia, with sly delight that her plot is working out so smoothly: "I've already told you once. Oscar says there is no coal at all."

Grandfather, insensitive to the fact that he is speaking of Julia's husband: "You mean to say that that idiot has let us run out of coal and never said a word to a soul?"

Julia snaps the trap shut: "He says he told you last week that we were running short, and you told him you'd give him a check next time he went to the inn. But then you never did."

Grandfather: "But that was last week. Why didn't the silly man remind me?"

Julia: "He says he did. On Monday, it was."

Grandfather, thrashing about, looking for a way out of his sorry predicament: "And I didn't give him a check?"

Julia: "No, Mr. Dunlap. You said you were busy and to wait till Tuesday."

Grandfather: "And now we haven't got a lump in the camp? All right, get Oscar immediately and I'll give him the check, and he can go for the coal this afternoon."

Julia, having won the skirmish, decides this is the moment to complete her victory: "Mr. Dunlap, do you mind if I make a suggestion? Busy as you are, wouldn't it make sense for me to order the coal with the groceries when we need it? Then you can make up for it when you give me the check for the household expenses at the end of the month."

Grandfather, noble as Lee at Appomattox: "An excellent idea, Julia. I don't know why we've never thought of it before."

Julia, unable to resist a victor's swagger: "I did, Mr. Dunlap. Last year when the same thing happened, I told you should let me order the coal."

Grandfather: "You did?"

Julia: "I did, Mr. Dunlap, and you said you'd think about it. But since you never said another word about it, I didn't think it was up to me to bring it to your attention."

Grandfather, having had enough of this puny insurrection, decides it's time to put Julia in her place: "Julia, I think it would be a good idea, don't you, if we had lunch promptly at twelve instead of twelve-thirty? I think Bud wouldn't get so cranky if we ate a little earlier."

Julia: "As you wish, Mr. Dunlap."

Grandfather: "Good. And do you think we might start today?"

Julia: "Yes, Mr. Dunlap, if that's what you wish. But lunch will be cold, you know. There's no coal for cooking."

This last remark is an unpleasant reminder that Grandfather cannot tolerate. "Yes, yes, I know. But I'll have to think about that idea of yours of putting the coal on the grocery bill at the inn. I don't want the bill there to get too high."

Julia doesn't dare spit out the word *shit* in Grandfather's presence, and so she exits in a frustrated huff of having had victory snatched from her at the last moment. Yet, as regularly happens, each protagonist has had his or her moment of triumph and left the field with honor intact.

SUCH COLLISIONS between Grandfather and Julia occurred two or three times a summer, particularly over the coal, which imposed on Oscar such Sisyphean labor as to excuse his periodically ignoring it. To get the coal at the Saranac Inn, he had to tow behind the Chris-Craft a large wooden barge originally used to deliver building materials to the camp. At the inn's dock he had to load the barge with eighty-pound canvas sacks of coal and then tow it at a snail's pace back to camp. Once there, he had to carry each filthy sack up the long flight of steps to the coal bin just outside the kitchen, dump it, then trot down for the next sack. It was a task that took a good seven or eight hours and left Oscar limp, black with coal dust, and exhausted.

The battles between Julia and Grandfather were wonderful to watch, each tacitly acknowledging the strict protocol of the polite confrontation between servant and employer. Also, because she was

Swedish, Julia was almost as respectable as an Anglo-Saxon. She was a good cook, as I have said, and she could persuade Oscar to shave every third day or so and me to mind my manners—an accumulation of virtues sufficient to mitigate the lèse-majesté of arguing with an honest to God, authentically fake Kentucky colonel.

CHAPTER TWO

I OFTEN THINK OF GRANDFATHER as a prototype of the twentieth century's prosthetic man, someone who would think nothing of checking into the hospital for new hips, knees, or kidneys. Though Grandfather was a bit too early for such handy replacement parts, to my child's eyes there seemed to be few organs in his body that modern medicine hadn't tinkered with. If he didn't have his cane, he walked with the lurching, staggering gait of Ahab in a typhoon. Shed of his toupee, his pate was as smooth and polished as an inverted chamber pot. He wore false teeth, was blind without his glasses, and was hard of hearing. Finally, because of a hernia, around his groin he wore a truss that he was continually adjusting.

Yet Grandfather was in no way a hypochondriac and carried off these afflictions, and their compensatory devices, with a panache that made me envious, hoping that one day I too might be blessed with them. To be sure, Grandfather seemed immensely old and sorely handicapped by his disabilities, but he had a style often lacking in today's geriatric set. He wielded his cane with flamboyance, using it as a goad for Oscar and slow-moving Pullman porters alike. With one good rap on the head he once silenced my four-year-old cousin, gone hysterical when the horn of the Chris-Craft briefly stuck. That cane was a pointer, lance, and quarterstaff with which he would alternately cajole, bully, or threaten anyone who had the temerity to stand in his way.

Only his toupee at all injured his sensibilities, and that went back to the day his doctor him to cover his pate permanently. In wintry or rainy weather, Grandfather, then in his sixties, was constantly being laid low by chills and fever. After careful diagnosis his doctor concluded that baldness was clearly the cause of his illnesses and ordered him to cover his head either with a skullcap or a toupee. Investigating the matter, Grandfather found that a suitable skullcap could be had for a dollar or so, whereas a single respectable toupee would set him back some three hundred dollars, even in the 1920s. Furthermore, to keep a toupee properly dry-cleaned and decent looking he would need at least two and preferably three. The solution was obvious: a skullcap. A day or two later, with the cap snug on his head, he repaired for lunch to his favorite restaurant in downtown Manhattan.

A methodical man, Grandfather was given to frequenting the same restaurant, barbershop, or shoeshine parlor for years on end. At this particular eatery he had a standing agreement with the headwaiter that no one with Jewish features should be seated near him at his favorite table by the window. Now, as could only happen by malevolent coincidence, on this day the regular headwaiter was absent. His place was taken by a simple, well-meaning fool unknown to Grandfather but fully cognizant of his instructions regarding acceptable dining neighbors. One glance at the skullcap and the unfortunate fellow was at Grandfather's elbow.

"I'm sorry, sir, this table is reserved."

"Reserved! Do you know, sir, who you are talking to?"

"I beg your pardon, sir, but I must insist. This table is already taken."

Grandfather's cane went into action, voices were raised, tempers flared. Grandfather demanded to see the regular headwaiter. Who was this insulting impostor? Where was the manager? All might have ended in fury had not Grandfather's regular waiter fortuitously appeared at the critical moment and signaled wildly to Grandfather, pointing to the skullcap. Grandfather caught the message. In a trice the cap was off.

Within days Grandfather had snipped off the bun on Grandmother's head and had it fashioned into several hairpieces at three hundred dollars each. Moreover, the story of the skullcap became a standard part of his repertoire at Thanksgiving and Christmas as he presided at the table, carving the turkey and pronouncing that there should be no question about it: the pope's nose was his.

AS A CHILD I did not discover the artful deceit of Grandfather's toupee until one torrid day in July when he removed it for his afternoon nap and neglected to put it back on. Sitting in the living room, I was amazed at this billiard-ball apparition. Later I grew quite accustomed to his baldness, as during heat waves he would strip off the toupee and sit on the verandah with a damp handkerchief draped over his head, looking for all the world like a desert pasha gone loony in the heat.

For all his infirmities Grandfather had one talent I shall forever envy: inserting his little fingers between his teeth, he could give forth an earsplitting whistle that could be heard a half mile away. This ability was invaluable for summoning me, far out on the lake, to lunch, or for beckoning Oscar front and center for the orders of the day. Grandfather tried without success to teach me the knack. The trick, I was convinced, lay either in his handsome, machine-made teeth or in the shape of his fingers. The tips of his thumbs, like the beak of a hawk, were curved so far back that when pressed they almost touched his wrists. Then, of course, there was the suspicion that my scrawny, narrow chest simply could not muster the lung power to blow such a mighty blast.

Actually, it was the combination of all his prosthetic devices, used in skillful concert, that set Grandfather apart from the common run of men. Meeting him for the first time could be an unnerving experience. Spotting his prey, Grandfather would walk across the room, rising and falling like an oil-well pump as he shifted from good leg to bad. He would set his cane at his hip, adjust his pince-nez, thrust out his lower jaw—there was no mistaking the false teeth—and with head tilted back would survey the stranger with condescension. He never waited for the formalities of introduction.

"I'm John Dunlap," he would say, thrusting out his hand. If the stranger had any poise left, Grandfather would immediately demolish it: "Sorry, I didn't get your name. Deaf as a post, you know."

Another ploy to make sure the new acquaintance should not soon forget John Dunlap was for Grandfather to sweep the person off into a corner and pump him for his opinions on Roosevelt, socialism, and the gold standard. For reasons I have never quite been able to determine, Grandfather started out the Roosevelt era as a dedicated New Dealer. Of course, in those days and in the company he kept, this stance was like expressing admiration for Caligula or Benedict Arnold. Nothing seemed to rejuvenate Grandfather's spirits so much as a good political cat-and-dog fight, and the subject of Roosevelt was a surefire spark for a brawl. Grandfather was captivated, I suspect, by Hyde Park and Roosevelt's Groton-Harvard background. He delighted in the president's patrician attitude and liked his idea of helping the downtrodden, even as he counted himself among the "economic royalists" Roosevelt was always attacking.

To Grandfather, the zest of quarreling was old age's substitute for sex. He fought incessantly with his sons—my uncles Boyce and Jack—with my parents, and with his fellow camp owners on Upper

Saranac Lake. But Grandfather's favorite antagonist was his oldest and dearest friend, Willie Graham, who had made and held on to a fortune acquired in copper. Mr. Graham was a solidly built, jovial man with a perpetually smiling, pudding face and a splendid bulb of a nose. Each summer he spent ten days or so on Upper Saranac, staying, out of self-preservation undoubtedly, at the Saranac Inn, across the lake from Woodwil. From there each morning at eleven, Oscar fetched him in the Chris-Craft in time for lunch and a good argument, followed by a game of rummy.

It seems to me that Grandfather and Mr. Graham fought about everything—Roosevelt, of course, but also the stock market, various public figures, and mutual acquaintances. But most of all, they fought over the game of rummy. With the same regularity that Grandfather fleeced me at dominoes and cribbage, Mr. Graham took Grandfather for whatever change and small bills he had on him. This steady drain of cash set up such resentment in Grandfather that Mr. Graham could not so much as blink without appearing to gloat.

"You just had a bad day, John," Mr. Graham would assure Grandfather as he stuffed bills in his wallet. "Wait till tomorrow; you'll win it all back." But this oil on troubled waters only created an explosive mixture, and on several occasions I remember Mr. Graham and Grandfather standing, respectively, at the boathouse and on the verandah of the main lodge, bellowing at each other that it was final; they never wished to see each other again. Then, with telephone calls and repentant, morning-after notes sent via Oscar, they made it up in time for the next day's lunch and argument.

In spite of his constant quarrels, Grandfather was convinced he had a snake charmer's way with people, especially with those he regarded as his social inferiors. Among waiters, storekeepers, bank tellers, and barbers, Grandfather moved with the grand manner of Napoleon reviewing the imperial guard. Usually he wove his spell by dropping a confidential word of personal concern and a ten-cent tip.

Whenever he found a barbershop or restaurant to his liking, he would unfailingly appear there for fifteen or twenty years, so that he came to know the complete family histories, pastimes, and interests of all the employees.

The black doorman at the Saranac Inn was one such presumed admirer, and when Oscar drove Grandfather up to the pillared porte cochere in Uncle Boyce's battered 1928 Buick sedan, Joe (Grandfather condescendingly named all black men Joe) would welcome him with the ruffles and flourishes due a field marshal. "Stand back, now," Joe would shout to the bellhops lounging about the entrance, "I'll get Colonel Dunlap's door." He would leap to the curb and with a hand at Grandfather's elbow assist him from the car. Grandfather, stepping from the unwashed, dent-disfigured automobile that Boyce had driven across the continent no fewer than four times, was totally oblivious to the absurdly pauperish ceremony of the occasion. Adjusting his truss with a tug at his groin, and with his cane hooked at the crook of his arm, he would search for change in his vest pocket. The dime was tendered royally.

"Thank you, Joe, thank you. And how's Mamie?" (Mamie was his name for every black female.) Grandfather shared the traditional southern view that only white men born below the Mason-Dixon line had any understanding of the childlike gentleness of the black man. After all, he was wont to boast, he himself had been weaned at the breast of his father's house slave in antebellum Kentucky, implying that this experience gave him a special understanding of black people.

With these pleasantries ritualistically observed, Joe would escort Grandfather into the lobby of the inn, the two of them head to head in an intense, secret conversation. Grandfather had somehow convinced Joe that their mutual burden was the successful management of the inn and the health of Harrington Mills, its 250-pound owner. Grandfather believed Mills was in mortal danger of a stroke brought on by the imminent bankruptcy of the inn combined with the perils of gluttony. Thus, at each meeting, during the short walk from the porte cochere to the lobby, Grandfather scrupulously queried Joe about the new arrivals at the inn, the present occupancy rate, and whether Mr. Mills had lately shown any evidence of thickness in his speech or palsy in his hands. The worse the news, of course, the more pleased was Grandfather, and in parting he would extract a solemn promise from Joe to look after Mr. Mills and to let Grandfather know immediately if there were any deterioration in Mills's health.

Actually, Grandfather's concern for Harrington Mills's well-being was not unique. My bowels were also a source of a compulsive interest to him. Breakfast each day included a hearty helping of prunes, which I detested, for us both. Grandfather was also a great believer in the efficacy of what he gutturally pronounced "roughage" in producing a beneficent intestinal tract. Every day I had to stuff away enough bran and other grainy cereals to make me whinny like a colt. Despite these palliatives, Grandfather apparently felt that my health was imperiled by constipation, and at lunch his first question was often, "Well, Bud, have your bowels moved?" At the slightest sign of peakedness he immediately ordered Julia to dose me with mineral oil.

Because his limp was the result of medical bungling, Grandfather had deep-rooted contempt for doctors. Besides mineral oil, he put his faith in a shot of whiskey and an occasional aspirin as cures for all bodily ills. A Hobbesian to the core, he believed passionately in the depravity of human beings so that no corruption or mean-spiritedness took him by surprise. Yet his humor was never far below the surface. He laughed for a week once when Oscar got drunk and in retaliation against Julia's bluenose propriety took the potbellied stove from the guidehouse where they lived and threw it into the lake. To Grandfather, this was an act of sublime rebellion, personifying the human folly in which he so profoundly believed. "Why, he'll only have Julia now to keep him warm," he said with glee at the no-tion of Oscar snuggling up to Julia. "But dammit, you've got to admit the man's got character after all."

GRANDFATHER, AS I HAVE SAID, spent his last years composing a genealogy of the Dunlap family. It was a work he did not live to finish, and certainly if he had, it would have been one of the more confused, disorganized books to see print. I still have the typescript of several chapters he completed, and from them I get the feeling that Grandfather went about writing the way W. C. Fields might have done his bookkeeping.

His method was to gather as many miscellaneous documents as he could lay his hands on—old letters, newspaper clippings, copies of land deeds, birth certificates—as well as numerous extensive quotes from books and historical figures he admired. Then, with paste pot and pen he tied the whole together in a patchwork of quotations, a few confirmed facts, and his own distinctive opinions and recollections. Interspersed with statements from Jefferson, William Pitt the Elder, Grant, Lincoln, and Henry Clay were paragraphs inveighing against George III, the Stamp Act, the Catholic Church, "the stupid German kings," and "the brainless British aristocrats." In Grandfather's eyes the world was variously peopled by tyrants, villains, and plain boobs—plus, of course, those noble creatures who were of the same virtuous stock as he.

Furthermore, factual evidence placed no constraints on Grandfather. The plan of the genealogy, for example, was simple. Each chapter was to be devoted to the remarkable career of a single distinguished ancestor, such as his great-great-grandfather, William Dunlap, who founded the Kentucky branch of the family when he moved his household from Virginia to the bluegrass region around Lexington in 1784. The problem was that these forebears' achievements were neither so notable nor so well documented that they suf-

ficed to fill more than a paragraph or two. Still, Grandfather was not
to be deterred: in a burst of imaginative historiography he arbitrarily
placed his ancestors at the very hub of the historical events occurring
within their lifetimes.

William, for example, did fight as an officer in the Revolution,
and one of Grandfather's proudest boasts was his membership in the
Society of the Cincinnatus, as the direct descendant of an officer in
Washington's army. But Grandfather, with his cavalier attitude toward historical fact, placed William in various campaigns and battles
on the spurious supposition that because William had held a commission in the Kentucky militia, and because the militia did con-
tribute troops to the Revolutionary army, he must have been
engaged in the actions cited. By the same reasoning, Grandfather
himself might well have been standing next to Teddy Roosevelt at
the taking of San Juan Hill.

In his father, Henry Clay Dunlap, however, Grandfather did have
an authentic Civil War hero. Standing six feet six, Henry was named
for the Great Pacificator, who had been his own father's best friend.
Joining the Kentucky Third Infantry in the summer of 1861, Henry
Clay Dunlap rose rapidly through the ranks, ultimately to be
breveted brigadier general commanding his regiment. In more than
three years of active service he fought in many of the major engage-
ments of the Kentucky and Tennessee campaigns, including Shiloh,
Chickamauga, and Mission Ridge, and ended his career commanding
the regiment on Sherman's March to the Sea. He was wounded once,
taking a musket ball in each thigh in a skirmish on the Green River
near Bowling Green, Kentucky, in 1862, and in his most notable act
of bravery he placed the Union flag atop the hill in the battle of Mission Ridge in November 1863.

Having survived the Civil War, the brave general died tragically.
His lands and fortunes destroyed by the conflict, he secured from
President Grant a post, at two thousand dollars a year, as storekeeper

of a bonded warehouse (the era's euphemism for revenue officer). In 1872, according to his class report at Jefferson College (today Washington and Jefferson College), "he was detailed to inspect a certain distillery whose owner's methods were suspected. In the discharge of his duty he discovered violations of the law. He was resisted, and in the encounter which followed the distiller struck him on the temple with a pistol, causing a fracture of the skull. Brain fever followed and on September 9, 1872, he died."

The sense of a glorious past was strong in Grandfather, and out of the muddled chapters of his genealogy a voice of passionate patriotism and genuine love of the land emerges. In old age he was a totally urban as well as urbane man who hardly knew the difference between a hemlock and a pine. He sneered at fishing as a "lily picker's" pastime and had no use for city people who, once in the Adirondacks, dressed as natives. Yet frozen in his stiff hip and arrogantly patrician manner was a nostalgia for the bluegrass and the simple, mythical virtues of the Kentucky frontier that led him to indulge my own childish passions. Transplanted to the Adirondacks, he encouraged my forays into the wilderness with a rare enthusiasm that made him lovable.

GRANDFATHER WAS WIDOWED for the first time in 1908, after which my mother, at the time only nineteen and the eldest of three children, was in charge of his household until her marriage in 1917. In a sense Grandfather lived a rather spartan life. He liked going to fine restaurants, socializing with rich men, and being seen in the right places, but he neither smoked nor drank, except for an occasional weak splash of whiskey before dinner, and at home he was oblivious to his furnishings and the fare at his table. These habits should have made housekeeping for him easy, even for an inexperienced girl. But with household money Grandfather was extremely tight, so that every six months or so panic reigned when all the creditors appeared at the door en masse. Then a conference with Mother ensued, during which Grandfather would examine the household accounts and roar at the extravagance of three meals a day and clean bedsheets once a week.

Perhaps Grandfather's strangest eccentricity was the way he traveled. On a business trip he never took along a suitcase, only a briefcase into which he crammed a toothbrush, razor, and comb. For the rest of his needs he lived off the land, buying a change of shirt, socks, tie, and underwear at various cities on his itinerary and sending home discrete parcels of dirty laundry as he went along. If offering no other advantage, this odd method of travel at least had the benefit of keeping his family informed of his whereabouts through the postmarks on the parcels of dirty laundry. By the end of a two-week trip his suit must have been a bit rumpled, but Grandfather had such flair that he could look elegant in long johns and slippers.

On the overnight train from New York City to Upper Saranac Lake, for example, Grandfather's stiff hip made it impossible for him to undress in the cramped Pullman berth. Thus, he lay all night, rigid with sleeplessness and fully clad except for his jacket, vest, and shoes. Yet when he stepped down onto the platform at Saranac Inn station and stood waiting for Oscar to collect his bags, he looked for all his dishevelment more impeccable than many a British dandy in Savile Row clothes.

In fact, looking back, it seems to me that Grandfather spent a good part of his life living off the land, as it were. He had seen hard times more than once. After the Civil War and following his father's death, he served as a surveyor's apprentice in the Shenandoah Valley, remapping the desolation General Sheridan had left behind. From there he found his way into the newspaper business, rising to general manager and editor of the *Louisville Commercial*. Eventually he made himself wealthy as a pioneer editor and publisher of trade and industrial magazines. *Iron Age, Industrial Management,* and, most intriguing of all, *India Rubber World* were some of the titles in the stable of publications he sold to McGraw-Hill in 1925.

But in addition to the climactic crash of 1929, he lost his shirt two other times, in the panic of 1908 and again soon after World War I, when his second son, Jack, persuaded him to sink a fortune into a business-oriented picture magazine—more than a decade before photography had come of age as a journalistic tool. Each time, Grandfather, living in effect out of his briefcase, pulled together from the dirty laundry of disaster sufficient clothing to appear his prosperous, dignified self again.

Even in his salad days Grandfather was forever pulling up stakes and selling off his property to move to another city in another part of the country. Long before he built Woodwil in the 1920s, he had built another camp on Upper Saranac in the early 1890s, just when the lake was beginning to gain a reputation as a summer resort. Here he raised his three children, only to sell the place immediately following World War I. Similarly, at one time he owned a house in Brooklyn and later one in Englewood, New Jersey, but moving each time for no apparent reason other than a desire for a change of scenery. He traveled widely, in Europe as well as in the United States, and visited Russia at the turn of the century. When the scandals of burst Russian dams and inefficient steel mills surfaced in the 1930s, that trip to Russia allowed him the I-told-you-so hindsight of exclaiming, "Why, dammit, what did you expect? When I was there in 1903 those Russians couldn't even make a hotel reservation." Throughout his travels, through wars, deaths, and financial disasters, Grandfather remained the bluegrass gentleman, sneering at the French, the "lily pickers," and the British aristocracy, and extolling Thomas Jefferson and Woodrow Wilson as the South's contribution to history's immortals.

When he was seventy-six or so, he became exasperated one hot summer day at the unsightly litter of tin cans that I had used for target practice with my .22 and that now lay sunken in the lake near the boathouse. Because Oscar couldn't swim and I had a cold (and undoubtedly was suffering from constipation), he decided to fish them out himself. At the time I don't think he had been swimming for twenty years, and, furthermore, the water in that spot was at least seven feet deep. Before descending to the boathouse, he told Julia she was not to leave the kitchen or peer out toward the lake for at least forty-five minutes. Retiring to his bedroom, he appeared a few minutes later stripped of everything—clothes, toupee, false teeth, glasses, and truss—except for his cane and a pair of ballooning, knee-length undershorts. He then limped down to the boathouse, where Oscar was stationed in a canoe to receive the cans once Grandfather had retrieved them from the lake bottom.

The first daunting obstacle to his can-collecting expedition was the means of getting into the water. With no swimming ladder at the boathouse, and his innumerable afflictions clearly precluding a head-first dive, his solution was inspired. With his cane probing in front of him like a mine detector, he gingerly inched and hobbled his way to the outermost edge of the floating canoe ramp, where he stood waiting, haughtily immobile as a biblical prophet, for the hinged ramp to slowly sink under his weight. When the water was waist high, he pushed out into the lake with a dignified breast stroke, letting his cane float away. Oscar and I were too stunned to laugh and too fearful and respectful to cheer.

After swimming to the spot above the cans, Grandfather solved the surface diving problem in a less spectacular but all the more marvelous fashion. He paddled about for a few moments, then blew the air out of his lungs, ducked his head, and like a strange white sea lion sank to the bottom. He grabbed a can in each hand and rose to the surface, his bald head breaking through the water in a blast of bubbles and exhaled breath. Five or six times he submerged, and when he had recovered and passed all the cans to Oscar, he swam back to the ramp. Here he sat down, and with his hands propelling him backward on his bottom inch by inch, he attained the safety of the boathouse.

The whole undertaking was an accomplishment richly deserving of his triumphant boasts. Standing in his dripping undershorts, his eyes smarting from the water, his baldness suddenly old and human, and his chin—usually arrogantly jutting with his false teeth—now shrunken to a small knob, he hugged a towel to his chest and bellowed, "By God, Bud, it takes an old man to get a job like that done." Then, blowing his nose on the towel, he barked at Oscar, "Oscar, dammit, did you get my cane? Are you an idiot? The thing will float away if you don't get it immediately."

God bless the old man: for all his bigotry and arrogance, in old age and lameness, sans teeth, hair, and decent sight and hearing, he went swimming at seventy-six to clean up the mess I at twelve had made, a mess that to him seemed intolerable on a Kentucky gentleman's estate.

 CHAPTER THREE

SOME TIME AGO I READ that the Adirondacks, according to at least one school of geologists, are the oldest mountains in the world, at one time towering as high as the Himalayas. I am not sure of the significance of this fact, except that it may afford gentlemanly Adirondackers such as Grandfather a smug sense of superiority. If the Adirondacks are indeed older than the upstart Himalayas or Rockies, they wear their age with a dark, shapely beauty unrivaled by other regions I have seen. Abraded by eons of wind, rain, snow, and ice, the low-lying mountains (the highest, Mount Marcy, is approximately 5,300 feet) are rounded and sculpted into slopes and valleys that lead the eye in long blue and green panoramas in every direction. Though wilder and less peopled than perhaps any other region on the eastern seaboard, the Adirondacks seem a peaceful landscape in which the countless lakes and ponds, the forest and gently sloping mountains, all lend the illusion that here lies that peculiarly American myth, the Happy Hunting Ground.

If Grandfather and his ilk were slightly addlepated over their wilderness retreats, just a glimpse of Upper Saranac or Blue Mountain Lake at sunset on a July evening, with the reflection of the sun a gold path across the water and the points of land nosing out into the lake like so many huge mythological beasts, can certainly make one understand their passion.

36

As testimony to its subtle beauty, it can be argued that few regions of the country have attracted the eyes of so many artists and painters. As early as 1837, in visiting the area around Schroon Lake, Thomas Cole and Asher Durand, the founding fathers of the Hudson River school, were stunned, in Cole's words, by the "sublimity of untamed wilderness, and the majesty of the eternal mountains." Cole and Durand were followed throughout the nineteenth century by a host of leading painters: Arthur Tait, John Kensett, and, most significant of all, Winslow Homer, who, besides his seascapes of Maine and the Caribbean, left an indelible mark on American art with his oils and watercolors of Adirondack life. The twentieth century also made its contribution with the work of such painters as Georgia O'Keeffe and John Marin, and of the sculptor David Smith, who created an outdoor gallery for his massive steel and metal constructions in the meadows overlooking Lake George.

And yet, for all its beauty, the Adirondack region is a harsh place. From Lake George north to the Canadian border the soil is hardly fit to grow a carrot. Unlike Vermont, just across Lake Champlain, where the Green Mountains have a similarly seductive female aspect, the Adirondacks boast few farms with classic white clapboard houses, red silos, and mountainside pastures dotted with cows. In winter the temperature regularly drops to well below zero and at times reaches minus forty degrees. But that is only half of it: snow piles up four and five feet deep, with drifts, driven by gale-force winds, deep enough to bury a good-size truck or single-story shack. Out on the lakes the ice freezes two or more feet thick, and unless shoveled, roofs regularly collapse under the weight of snow and ice.

But winter is only one facet of the harshness of the Adirondack climate. Hard frosts are not unusual in August, and well before Labor Day some years ago the peak of Whiteface Mountain, the main site of Lake Placid's Olympic skiing events, wore a mantle of dusted snow. And then there's the rain. In the Adirondacks it doesn't simply rain and then, after a good downpour, have the decency to stop. For days on end the sky can weep and sob interminably, collecting all the gray clouds east of the Great Lakes and massing them to parade in disorderly regiments through the mountains.

I remember one summer with Grandfather when, so help me, it rained twenty-seven out of the thirty days in June. True, it did not pour uninterruptedly for those twenty-seven days, or like Noah we would have taken to the Chris-Craft to float our way to the peak of Marcy. But each day brought either an hour's teeming downpour, with thunder crashing and reverberating off the mountain slopes, or a daylong hissing drizzle that confined me to fishing under the eaves of the boathouse and Grandfather to limping back and forth in grumbling frustration between the fireplace and his desk. "Dammit, Bud, in all my years I have never seen weather like this in the Adirondacks," he would say each day at lunch. But, of course, every year in one way or another seems like no other year.

Rounding out this litany of woe are the bugs, most especially the infamous blackflies and gnats (charmingly called "nosee'ums") that have made a legend of the Adirondacks. In early June, at about nine in the evening, not long after the sun has set, if you have nerves of steel, you should sit outside in the soft night air and listen to the insects rising from the forest floor. A faint hum at first, it mounts to a high, thin whine that penetrates the ear like a cold wire. All at once you realize your whole head and body are ringing like a tuning fork to the unearthly hum of millions of insects.

In the face of this menace Grandfather was, to say the least, either monstrously deluded or just plain blockheaded. In those days there were insecticides such as Flit and also citronella. The former Grandfather dismissed as an oily, evil-smelling concoction that didn't really do any good, and the faintest whiff of the latter sent him into inexplicable paroxysms of revulsion. His solution to the bug problem was typically high-handed: either keep out of their way by staying indoors or, like the Indians, ignore them. (As with his theories about blue blood, Grandfather was convinced, on the basis of some never-specified authority, that Indians were immune to insect bites.)

His convictions put me, at ages twelve and thirteen, through torture because in emulation of Uncas and other Mohican braves I felt impelled while out in the woods to expose myself to as many feasting blackflies and mosquitoes as possible. As a consequence, throughout June, the height of blackfly season, I was one red welt of bug bites. Julia constantly applied camphor ice, but I am not sure it did much good. Certainly, for all my prayers to the ghost of Uncas, the torturous immunization process Grandfather advocated never so saturated my blood that I could walk in the woods unscathed. But I suspect the continual itching and scratching at least made me feel closer to Oscar, who was also continually itching and scratching (though owing more to neglect in applying soap, no doubt, than to bug bites).

With such a climate it is no wonder that the Adirondacks are a poor region. Aside from lumbering, sharply reduced since the creation of the Forest Preserve just prior to the turn of the century and even more so with the establishment of the Adirondack Park Agency in the early 1970s, there are few sources of stable, year-round employment. Tourism remains the bread and butter of the economy, but come October, that work vanishes. Lack of income is everywhere reflected in sad, decaying towns, cramped houses, and mobile homes set on cinder blocks as permanent residences. Even Saranac Lake village, which during the heyday of the world-famous Trudeau tuberculosis sanatorium (roughly from 1885 through World War II) boasted it was one of the most cosmopolitan communities of any town its size, today appears diminished by the disease that made its reputation.

Fortunately, through the efforts of the APA (as the Adirondack

Park Agency is known) and various citizen organizations, the Adirondacks as a whole have been spared much of the commercial blight that afflicts the American landscape elsewhere. In the main, a drive through the Adirondacks remains a miraculous unfolding of nature's magnificence, and the Northway especially, the main artery joining Albany and Montreal, serves as a triumphal causeway through scenery beautiful enough to mitigate the worst of mans' desecrations.

Grandfather was no environmentalist or even conservationist, if indeed he had ever heard of such callings. Yet in his way he did genuinely love nature; that is, he loved nature tamed. His ideal was the lordly English estate—not the duke of Devonshire's Chatsworth, perhaps, but a commodious house, staffed by upstairs and downstairs maids, with stables, a manicured private park, and a trout stream. In his last years, as the stranglehold of the Depression dimmed his hopes of recouping his fortune through land development, Grandfather decided in despair to sell the whole kit and caboodle, Woodwil included. With his inimitable editorial style he put together a sales brochure, complete with photographs and appropriate captions. The camp, he wrote, "has been deliberately planned after the English system of household management. That is to say, the Servants Quarters, Kitchen and Laundry are OFF TO THEMSELVES. This means the servants have their own household, their own assembly rooms and their dock on the waterfront—all of which makes for domestic peace and contentment."

On a modest scale, Woodwil reflected Grandfather's dream of the English-style estate. When he bought the fifty acres of peninsula jutting out into Upper Saranac, the land was in the wild state the Adirondack Park was created to preserve: virgin forest full of magnificent stands of giant hemlock, pine, and spruce, with thickets of scrub and fallen trees, hummocks of rotten stumps, bogs, and high rock ledges. All this, Grandfather decreed, should be transformed into an expanse of tamed and cultivated woodland where—amid towering trees, across a forest floor as raked and stickless as an English gentleman's park, along paths lined with white birch saplings—he could escort small parties of wellborn and properly awestruck guests.

I suspect that Grandfather was inspired in his undertaking by the private deer park that a member of the Blagden family of New York had established around the turn of the century. At the time I knew the deer park, it was owned by one of the Severance family of Cleveland. It was located a mile or so from the Saranac Inn and consisted of a roughly thirty-acre tract of woodland that had been properly tamed and cleared and stocked with a hand-fed herd of deer and other assorted wildlife. The park was ringed the whole way around with a ten-foot-high wire-mesh fence. Visits were by invitation only, and I can dimly remember going there with my grandparents in the late twenties, before my summerlong stays with Grandfather.

In my Sunday best—short trousers, kneesocks, and sailor blouse with a black neckerchief worn, oddly, in memory of Lord Nelson—I would trot several steps ahead of Grandfather and his wife as we joined a select few ladies and gentlemen from the inn and other camps on the lake, sedately indulging in vicarious enjoyment of the world of Daniel Boone and Natty Bumppo. To maintain the park in an appropriately tamed state, two full-time men, plus a superintendent, trimmed and tended the forest till toddlers and old folks alike could walk about without fear of tripping on anything larger than a twig.

The visits were a formal occasion, the men in pinstriped white trousers, light summer jackets, and Panama hats or straw boaters, the ladies in long pastel-colored dresses and cartwheel-size summer hats fit for archery targets. Although Grandfather and his wife, Isadora, walked at a leisurely pace, I was continually getting underfoot, so that Grandfather was forever prodding me with his cane:

"Get a move on, Bud, get a move on." In an hour I am sure we covered no more than a quarter mile, following the winding paths of the park and nodding to acquaintances or stopping for a chat. Then, alas, we ended the afternoon by taking tea at the inn, where a string quartet on the broad verandah entertained the exhausted walkers.

A deer park with a ten-foot wire fence was beyond Grandfather's means even in his most affluent days. But with his genius for cutting corners, he hired George Donaldson as his unofficial park superintendent and construction supervisor. In full recognition of the naïve, wide-eyed exaggeration of childhood, I still assert that George Donaldson in his prime—he was twenty-four or twenty-five at the time—was the strongest man to walk the earth. His biceps, I promise you, were as big as the average man's thighs and his forearms the size of a prime leg of lamb, with veins that in my envious eyes stood out like hawsers. In fact, George's whole body was so packed with muscle that when he bit into a sandwich cords of sinew stood out along his jaw, and in the simple act of chewing his face visibly widened. To clinch the matter, I once saw George pick up the rear end of Uncle Boyce's rattletrap Buick when it slid off the camp road and in three quick jolts heave it back.

During the depression years, when Grandfather persisted in pursuing his park project more as a lure to prospective buyers than as a dream of upper-class English gentility, he kept a careful record of expenses. He paid George, with the enlightened generosity of a Spanish conquistador, eighteen dollars a week. There were four other men in the crew, including at various times George's three brothers, Clifford, Adrian, and Harold, and each got twelve dollars a week—a week, by the way, that often lasted fifty hours or more. The entire payroll for five men was only sixty-six dollars. Thus, over the course of a summer the project cost less than $600, a sum that Grandfather in his straitened circumstances felt to be a cruel load and that prompted numerous conferences with George over cost-cutting measures. Might the men, for example, accept a cut in wages if Grandfather fed them lunch? (Julia put a quick stop to that nonsense.) Or might Oscar, in whose hands an ax was more danger to his own life than to any tree, be put to some use?

If George was superintendent of the project, I was the runner, liaison, and, I fear, unwitting spy between Grandfather and the crew. Only about every third or fourth day did Grandfather, with all the ceremony of Ferdinand de Lessees inspecting work in progress on the Suez Canal, emerge from the main lodge to check on his evolving park. He would confer with George on what trees should be removed, what alternative routes the birch-lined paths might follow, the placement of steps on inclines, and other matters of pith and moment. On these visits I always skipped ahead of him on the path, babbling away about what marvelous changes in the forest he should anticipate seeing since he last visited and about the latest feats of strength and axmanship by various members of the crew. Similarly, at lunch each day I was full of gossipy information about what the men had said, comments in which I am sure Grandfather took no end of interest.

In those days there were no gasoline-powered chain saws. The work was done with axes, two-man saws, and timber hooks. As I remember, the crew worked in revolving shifts, two men felling trees with the big-bladed two-man saws and two trimming the felled trees and dragging away the brush. In a good morning's work the crew could level fifteen trees, clear away scrub pine and balsam, and stack great piles of brush. After a successfully destructive morning, they would turn in the afternoon to carting off firewood from felled trees, sawing stumps to ground level, and raking up wood chips and sawdust.

For all this activity I was a fascinated sidewalk superintendent. Hopping about from stump to stump, retrieving here an ax temporarily laid aside, now using the end of a fallen tree as a springboard, I was one obsessive, continual question: What was the age of that tree? Why was hemlock so heavy? Did people really chew "spruce gum" like Doublemint or Juicy Fruit? (If they did, they must have had the discriminating taste of groundhogs.) Periodically, George or one of the men would stop in his work and, hunching over in exasperation, hands crossed on the butt of his ax, would state in an infinitely patient voice that if I didn't shut up, he'd drop a tree on me or jam his ax right down that big yap of mine—a threat I took, of course, as a hilarious compliment to my importance and indispensability.

Then there were the feats of strength and woodsmanship. At twelve or thirteen I was remarkably impressed by the physical prowess of anyone who could lift more than ten pounds off the ground, and needless to say, I was so in awe of the five mastodons of the crew that had one of them torn a mature hemlock out by the roots, I would have accepted the feat as just another demonstration of his godlike powers. Off and on throughout the day, I would challenge George or one of his brothers to drop a tree with five more blows of his ax or with one hand to lift a log I could not budge with a timber hook. On only one count did I have the better of them, and this I never let them forget: for all their strength and skill, not one brute among them could swim a stroke, and, indeed, as I later found out, they stood in mortal terror of water much above their waists.

The most exciting events of the work were the huge bonfires used to burn the brush from felled trees. Some of this brush was pulled out of sight behind a rock ledge, but two or three times a summer, with a permit from the park rangers, the crew would set fire to the immense piles they had stacked during a two—or three-week period. They made their fires on a rock cliff next to the lake so that if the fire got out of control, it could be pushed over the edge into the water. After a thorough sprinkling with kerosene, the slash was set afire, the first flames licking up through the twigs and needles with a popping, snapping heat that reeked of turpentine and coiled away in acrid black smoke. In no time the pile was like a blast furnace, burning with a roaring rush of flame and warming our faces twenty feet away with a glow almost hot enough to singe hair. As the flames mounted, the brush would suddenly collapse here and there in a small explosion that sent a shower of sparks and burning twigs arcing out to land on the bare rock or to extinguish in the lake below.

Within twenty minutes or so the fire would begin to sink. Then came what to me was the most thrilling part: the moth-and-candle game of leaping in among the still-hot embers, grabbing an unburned stick, and flinging it onto the heap of smoldering coals. Within minutes the soles of my boots would be in a fine state of charred gooeyness and my trousers and shirt, never mind my hands and face, were sufficiently filthy with grime to send Julia into hand-wringing ululations of Swedish female martyrdom.

In this manner the park took shape during two summers, with eighteen to twenty acres laid out in paths and woodland vistas. At Grandfather's direction every path led eventually to one or more of the building lots along the north shore of his peninsula. George and his crew took special care in clearing these lots, even building temporary wooden docks on the lakeshore, which could be reached in several instances by long flights of stairs.

When his trap was properly baited, with every enticement except half-clad Lorelei lounging seductively on anchored floats, Grandfather in a series of gracious Saturday luncheons invited members of the real estate profession from as far away as Lake Placid and Blue Mountain Lake to inspect the broad sweep of the lake, the woodland park, and, of course, the building sites. In those Depression years, sad to say, these stratagem never worked. But I suspect no salesperson from P. T. Barnum to Lee Iacocca hawked his wares with louder boast or more expansive claims. In a mimeographed flyer directed at real estate agents Grandfather trumpeted the beauties of his "Private Park of forty-three acres, with miles of leveled pathways, affording the most delightful walks amid towering forest trees, and leading off into thousands of square miles of the great Adirondack Forest Preserve." To whet the sportsman's appetite, he wrote that "a friend who spent a year in South Africa and brought home a roomful of big game trophies, tells me that it requires more actual skill to stalk and bag an Adirondack deer than any specimen of big game that ever came out of Africa."

What Grandfather failed to gain in cash, he took in admiration. In one of his scrapbooks he preserved a clipping from the _Adirondack Daily Enterprise_ of June 1, 1931, describing a visit by the humorist and writer Irvin S. Cobb to Woodwil: "Just before leaving [Saranac Lake village], Cobb drove over to Upper Saranac to call on his old friend, John R. Dunlap, who was also born and raised in Kentucky. There was of course much talk of old times in Kentucky, and in particular Cobb said: 'Dunlap, you have given me a breath of fresh Kentucky air. You don't need anything in this Adirondack camp, but a hound dog to sleep under the front porch."

AS IT TURNED OUT, the woodland park was only the opening gambit in Grandfather's sales campaign. Brooding on the failure of his efforts, he decided in a leap of inspiration that the reason buyers had not broken down the doors was not because the population was paupered by the depression, as he had been, but because his property was water locked—there was no road to link the camp with civilization. Once this premise had taken shape, Grandfather was determined to lay a road over three miles of nearly impenetrable forest and swamp, a tract that might have daunted the Army Corps of Engineers. His first overtures to local contractors were, to say the least, discouraging. Of the four or five contractors he approached, the lowest bid was $110,000, a figure that, considering the obstacles to be overcome, seems low almost to the point of bankruptcy even in 1932 dollars.

Grandfather's next brainstorm was so short of genius as to be certifiable idiocy. At that time, Roosevelt, with Harry Hopkins in charge, was in the process of launching the Works Progress Administration (WPA) to put money in the hands of the ill fed, ill clothed, and ill housed. As might be expected of a man of his entrepreneurial bent, Grandfather knew Hopkins slightly. With a less than keen understanding of the proper separation of the public and private sectors, Grandfather wrote Hopkins, proposing that the federal government, with WPA manpower and funds, should build his private road. After all, he reasoned, the unemployed were going to be put to work anyway, often on projects, such as spearing trash in public parks, that would generate no further capital or economic growth. Why not assign them to a project that held such spangled promise of land development, tourist promotion, and a host of other enterprises? Needless to say, Hopkins did not see the matter that way, and here began, I suspect, Grandfather's growing disillusion with the New Deal and the squire of Hyde Park.

At length Grandfather turned, as he had with his woodland park project, to the stalwart shoulders and mighty biceps of George Donaldson. The scheme they worked out was a masterpiece of Kentucky horse trading. Grandfather would buy George a dump truck and give him $10,000 (some in the family have the sum as $30,000) to cover all costs of building the road. Today, no matter which figure is cited, the agreement sounds like thievery. But to Grandfather's credit, he measured his man well, for the truck, with the money left over from the project—and George actually did turn a profit—gave George a start that he parlayed over the years into a small fortune.

I was not witness to much of the construction because the project began far back on the mainland, and much of the work was done in fall and spring, when Woodwil was empty and George and his crew had completed more profitable summer jobs. Astonishingly, the road took only two years to build, but to Grandfather's woe (though to my own and my family's joy ever since) the project led to yet another dead end in his dreams of land speculation. Today, more than fifty years later, the road is still in use. After some periods of neglect when it nearly sank back into the swamp over which much of it is built, it is now in better shape than ever in its long life. Each year, under an agreement among the five current property owners, truckloads of large stone are laid down on the roadbed. Over the years three bridges spanning slow-moving streams have been replaced and rebuilt, until now they are constructed of sixteen-inch steel I-beams overlaid with heavy hemlock planking. In a sense, though, the road is more like a wilderness track, wide enough for only one car and winding through swamp and forest across a landscape as wild as any on the eastern seaboard.

To my mind the Adirondacks only really begin with the turn off the highway onto this old road. Suddenly the forest closes in, damp and redolent with the spiced smell of evergreen, and the view is blocked barely ten feet from the track by a wasteland of trees, broken now and then by wide vistas of desolate swamp. Though just more than three miles long, the trip from end to end takes a good twenty minutes and often longer when the area is flooded after a heavy rainstorm. The car brushes through overhanging boughs, down steep inclines, and noses around blind turns where occasionally a deer or ruffed grouse may be startled into flight. In the road's final stretches the lake appears through the fingered forest. The ground rises, and the driver glides beneath the columned heights of the few giant hemlock and spruce that remain of Grandfather's woodland park, a park murderously decimated by lumbering in the late 1940s.

The myth of American innocence dies hard. Without being sentimental, it existed here once, during my childhood, in the glory of this land. Most of Grandfather's park is now a jungle of stunted trees that will take decades before the fittest will thin out to tall forest. A lesser evil is the road. Ironically, it is now the old man's monument, bequeathing, as no amount of cash from his failed development schemes ever could have done, a quiet refuge and retreat to successive generations.

"The sportsmen and young people," he wrote, "love the forest, the lakes and the out-of-doors, but the ladies and the old folks must have the physical comforts of home. And here we have both. . . . Living amid such surroundings is precisely like actual camping in the woods except that the ladies have baths, showers and stationary wash stands, with hot and cold water, and if they want to put on evening gowns for social functions, they can do so quite as securely as in a Newport villa."

CHAPTER   FOUR

GRANDFATHER ALWAYS INSISTED that the seven-mile-long Upper Saranac was the largest lake in the Adirondacks. And, indeed, if you accepted his definition of the Adirondacks, which excluded out of hand Lake George (located in the "lily-picker" foothills) and Lake Champlain (really part of Vermont), and if you ignored seven other bodies of water, he was right. But Upper Saranac was his lake, and he was as jealously possessive of every inch of water and stick of wood bordering it as if he had given birth to it all with the tip of his finger.

Regardless of its size, on a large-scale map Upper Saranac looks like the one inkblot on a Rorschach test in which no person, however perverse, might discern an erotic image. There is just no sex at all in its squiggly, amorphous shape. At the extreme northern and southern ends there are large, open bodies of water that spread out in a disorderly, undisciplined manner. These two bodies are joined by a long, canal-like stretch—the Narrows—from which deep, narrow bays wander off to both right and left. And just to break up any semblance of symmetry, the entire lake is dotted with dozens of islands, some no more than lone rocks, others imposing tracts heavily forested and rising in rocky cliffs twenty and thirty feet above the water.

It is this shapelessness and irregularity that gives Upper Saranac its singular beauty. Except for Woodwil's five-mile view down through the Narrows, there is not another stretch of the lake where one can look across an expanse of water for more than a mile and a half. As a result, a trip by boat up its length is a continual series of surprises to the first-time visitor, who cannot help being charmed by the privacy of bays that at first appear to be separate lakes or ponds. As they travel farther, newcomers discover yet other small ponds, and so it goes until they reach the farthest end of the lake and are challenged to find their way home again. "My God!" they will exclaim. "Only someone who has lived here for years could possibly know his way through this maze." This is true; with the forest crowding right to the shoreline, each landmark looks familiar and each point like the one passed only five minutes earlier.

At its deepest spot the lake bottom lies one hundred feet below the surface, and many shoreline cliffs drop abruptly into ten or fifteen feet of water. But there are also sand beaches where a swimmer can wade out a hundred yards from shore with the water not much above his waist. Fortunately, the state owns extensive stretches of the land bordering the lake as part of the Forest Preserve, which means that at night as you travel by boat, for long periods you will have no light to steer by.

Then there are the shorelines populated by villages of camps, some discreetly hidden from the water by trees and the camouflage of rustic architecture, others blatantly obtrusive in suburban, split-level style. All are identifiable by their boathouses. Those built since World War II are usually no more than sheds set up on stilts, with a simple pulley contraption to raise boats out of the water for the winter. But boathouse building, as Grandfather said of Kentucky log cabins, "was carried to a fine art" in the days before the great crash of 1929. It was a time when millionaires, floating on gushers of oil or "watered" stock, outdid one another in erecting lavish pavilions. Three or four boat slips would be topped by an expansive sundeck and a coyly dubbed "playroom" more likely to be used by adults for

martinis and highballs than by children for Ping-Pong. The whole
would be gaily trimmed out with window boxes of geraniums and
petunias, with flagpoles and life rings lettered with the camp's name.

As a standing ritual, Grandfather gave guests a tour of the lake on
the evening of their first visit to Woodwil, with Oscar at the wheel of
the Chris-Craft. The entire trip was taken at full throttle, except
when Grandfather, to impress his guests with the quality of his
neighbors, would order Oscar to slow down for a leisurely inspection
of a Rockefeller, Bache, or Du Pont camp. For the rest, we rocketed
down the lake at full speed, sending a great rooster tail arcing from
our stern and leaving a wake behind us steep enough to put a canoeist in danger of capsizing—and furiously aware that it was the
Dunlap boat going by. Grandfather, as the patriarch, felt no compunction about taking the front seat beside Oscar in the shelter of
the windshield, generously yielding to his guests the exhilaration of
the cool evening air whipping about their ears and down their necks
as we sped along at thirty-five or forty miles an hour. Using his cane
as a pointer and with his free hand clapped atop his hat, he bellowed
out his tour guide's spiel in a voice loud enough to frighten small
children and cow adults into proper reverence for the grand sights
they were passing.

If Grandfather had had his way, water traffic on the lake would
have been limited to canoes and guideboats—except, of course, for
his own Chris-Craft, the *Arodasi*. Every time we passed another
powerboat on one of these tours, Grandfather would immediately
shout at Oscar: "Look out for the wake, now, Oscar, look out!"

Meekly Oscar would reply, "Yes, Mr. Dunlap. I see it, Mr.
Dunlap."

"But you're not turning fast enough. We'll get soaked unless you
meet it head-on."

The wake was usually still fifty yards away, but obediently Oscar
would turn and throttle down until we were nearly dead in the water.

Then, while we gently rocked back and forth as the menacing wake passed, Grandfather would reassure his guests that there was no cause for alarm; Oscar was a Swede and, as such, an experienced seaman—a prevarication the likes of which would have made Ananias pale with guilt. As a host Grandfather took his responsibility for the life, limbs, and well-being of his guests with a chilling solicitude. His concern was akin to that of the doctor who tells his patient that although his health is splendid, he should nevertheless forswear all pleasures of the flesh, drink, and table lest his heart give out at any instant.

Before each trip Grandfather would inspect the boat to make sure there was a life preserver or kapok flotation cushion for every passenger and each male in the party was assigned a helpless female to rescue in the event of disaster. Also, Oscar was grilled about the amount of gasoline in the boat and whether the running lights were in proper order, even though there was no chance of our returning to camp after nightfall. It was a wonder we didn't have boat drills and CPR instruction. Nor do I exaggerate. Well aware of the fame of the Trudeau tuberculosis sanatorium in nearby Saranac Lake village, and no doubt with an eye to the ravages of that disease, Grandfather reassured prospective buyers in one of his sales brochures: "The famous Trudeau sanitarium is twenty miles away from us [the accurate figure is twelve miles, but twenty, I suppose, was safely beyond the lethal range of the tuberculosis bacillus], and the hotels on our lake exclude tubercular patients so rigorously and so frankly, that they stay away from us severely, because it is so perfectly evident that they are not wanted."

IF JULIA'S FIEFDOM was the kitchen, Oscar's was the boathouse—not that he knew much about boats, engines, fishing, or other matters relating to the water. In all the years he worked for Grandfather, he never learned to land the Chris-Craft properly. Our boathouse was located in the elbow of a curving arm of rock projecting out into the lake. In order to land without being dashed against the slip by his own wake, the driver had to round the point in a tight turn and then head directly into the boathouse, reversing the engine at the last moment to avoid ramming the end of the slip.

Oscar, in his inimitably craven way, never had the nerve to make the tight turn and then stop the boat with the reverse as it entered the slip. Instead, he invariably took a wide turn and approached the boathouse at such a gingerly speed that he would be caught in his own wake. Then, in a frantic scramble, with the boat pitching and yawing amid the slosh and splatter of backwash, he would attempt to fend off the boat from the dock with a paddle or boat hook, swearing throughout (assuming, of course, that Grandfather was not present): "Oh, goddamn, son of a bitch, good Jesus Christ alive, if this boat gets a hole in it, I'll sink the fucking bastard!"

Officially, Oscar was Grandfather's guide. In the nineteenth century and even as late as the 1920s, an Adirondack guide was a respected, even venerated, figure. We see him most clearly in the paintings of Winslow Homer: the lean, wiry physique, dressed in coarse wool trousers, the flannel shirt buttoned to the neck, the suspenders, the battered hat. Usually he is posed in a canoe, following the path of his fly cast as the line curls out over the water, or in the forest, one foot on a fallen tree, an ax or rifle leaning against his hip. The guide is Homer's idealized primitive, wise in the ways of the wilderness—and, as a paid professional, indispensable to the rich, city-bred camper. He knows the deep pools where the big trout hide, the feeding grounds of the deer. In the "rough camp" he can pitch the tents, build the fires, and cook the meals of fresh-caught fish and flapjacks that give his well-heeled patrons the illusion of life in the wild.

Alas, Oscar had none of these qualities. By the 1930s, this breed of professional Adirondack guide had all but died out, a victim, as Grandfather would have said, of lily-picker tourism. However pretentious his title, Oscar was at best a handyman and not a very handy one at that. He felt at home in the boathouse, I suspect, because he had such a natural affinity for grease and grime. Unless his fingernails, hands, and clothes were black with filth, he did not feel a whole man. He was forever tinkering with the boat engines, not to tune or repair them; the workings of the internal combustion engine were as foreign to him as the ventricles of the heart. No, his was the curiosity of a small boy pulling apart an old-fashioned windup alarm clock: he simply liked the sight of the components laid out on a tarpaulin on the boathouse floor. The mere fact that he could take the tin boat's engine apart and put it back together again gave him, I am sure, a feeling of expertise otherwise absent from his character.

The tin boat, which was Oscar's favorite as well as mine, was a large, double-ended, dorylike craft sheathed in heavy tin. It had been purchased secondhand as a tow boat to haul the barges laden with building materials for Woodwil's construction. As such, it was sufficiently ungainly, slow, and presumably unsinkable as to be considered safe for me as a child. But there was a soul to this machine— hidden in its ponderous cast-iron one-lunger engine—and a vicious one at that. To begin with, it was the devil to start. First you had to prime it with gasoline, loosening the priming cup on top of the cylinder. Then you had to feed it gas with an oilcan while turning the flywheel, so that it sucked in the fuel with the slurping sound of a drunkard relishing his first shot of whiskey. This done, you advanced the spark and spun the flywheel, nerving yourself with a silent prayer that it wouldn't kick back and break your arm.

Another remarkable feature of the boat was that if you rapidly retarded and then advanced the spark while under way, the engine would go into reverse. But more astonishing than the bizarre method of accomplishing reverse gear was the drama enacted within the engine. Putting the engine into reverse appeared to inflict an agonizing pain and suspense on it, beginning with sporadic wheezes and hiccoughs, and mounting to snorts and farts of torturous discomfort that sent smoke-filled bubbles burbling up from the underwater exhaust. For a split second the engine appeared about to expire entirely, only to give forth a tremendous shudder that shook the boat from stem to stern before it leapt to life again in a frenzy of vibration at finding itself going backward instead of forward. Not surprisingly, given these fearsome characteristics, the engine terrified me. Oscar usually started it for me, whirling the flywheel and then, because there was no neutral, quickly leaping out as the boat started out of the slip. Still, the engine was so cantankerous that it often took even Oscar ten to fifteen minutes to get it started.

Oscar's love-hate relationship with the tin boat reached a crisis one hot July day when, after toiling away at the flywheel until his shirt was wringing wet with sweat, he sat down on the gunwale and took to swearing at the engine in a hopeless despair of frustrated love: "You goddamned son of a bitch of a tin bastard! Christ, I'd like to take a sledgehammer to that fucking cast-iron engine of YOURS!" He thrust out his leg from his perch on the gunwale as though to kick the engine, but instead he put his foot on the handle of the flywheel and gave it an angry shove. Believe me when I say that engine had Satan as a soul, for in as nasty a trick as the devil's own, it kicked back and flipped Oscar as deftly as a teeterboard, sending him head over heels into the lake. It happened too quickly for Oscar even to swear.

The next thing I knew he was clinging to the side of the boat, shouting, "Jesus, Bud, get me to the dock! Christ Almighty, that goddamned boat will drown me yet." Fortunately the boathouse was only twenty feet or so away, and I paddled the boat in with Oscar gripping the gunwale in peril of his life lest the engine fiendishly start up and cut off his legs with the propeller.

For all his fear of the water and ignorance of mechanics, Oscar was at one with Ratty in *The Wind in the Willows:* he believed there is nothing in life like "messing about in boats." The Chris-Craft in particular possessed him. He might not have been able to land that boat with any skill, but on its mahogany and bright work—the chrome knife edge of its bow, the windshield, cleats, and bumper eyes—he lavished all the cleanliness in polish and wax that was so patently lacking in his own being.

Occasionally I would catch Oscar alone in the boathouse with the hatch open, just sitting and doting on the engine's immaculate perfection. Once or twice during the summer, when he noticed a murmur in the firing of the pistons, he would summon the Gladd brothers from Saranac Lake village to tune the engine. While they labored away, Oscar would hop around the boathouse in a state of nerves or peer over their shoulders into the sanctity of the engine bay as though he expected at any moment to hear a strangled cry and see one of the brothers hold up a tiny infant Chris-Craft. When the job was done, Oscar would call me over, and the two of us would go out for a short spin to make sure the engine had survived its ordeal and was now purring in a state of perfect health and vibrancy.

The only evils in the Eden of Oscar's boathouse were the huge water spiders that nested on the underside of the boards lining the boat slips. These monstrous creatures, hairy and black, striped with yellow, and five or six inches across, would occasionally scoot out across the water or duck out from under the slip just as Oscar was stepping down into the outboard or tin boat. Their appearance was invariably followed by a gargled shriek from Oscar: "*Aaaugh!* Oh, good Jesus Christ, a spider! A paddle, Bud, quick, a paddle!"

I was as frightened of the spiders as Oscar, and as soon as I could grab two paddles from the canoe or dunnage closet, the two of us would lay about us, flaying the surface of the water in a radius five feet around the fearsome spider. On the rare instances when we suc-

ceeded in killing one, Oscar, as the braver of the two cringing cow-
ards, would scoop up the corpse on the blade of his paddle and lay it
on the boathouse floor, where, kneeling with our heads together, we
could probe it with a screwdriver.

"Jesus, Bud," Oscar would say, turning over the dead beast with
the point of the screwdriver, "one of these bastards could take a hunk
out of you as big as a fifty-cent piece. Christ, Bud, think if you found
that in your bed!" Both of us were as tense as coiled springs and ready
at the slightest sign of life to leap away in terror. But once we had
poked the spider enough to ensure that it was genuinely dead, Oscar
took a lively scatological interest in it.

"Where do you think it shits, Bud? Or does it shit? Christ, you
never know with these goddamned animals. Maybe it just gets bigger
and bigger until it explodes."

Oscar was mortally afraid of everything. During those rare heat
waves in July and early August when the hot, still air was a blue haze
on the distant surface of the lake, thunderstorms would regularly
mass over the mountains late in the afternoon. Uncharacteristically,
I was fascinated by the storms and would stand in the boathouse
watching the dark, rolling clouds move up the lake through the Narrows. But Oscar would panic. At the sight of the first thunderhead he
would take refuge in the kitchen, and only a manic loyalty to me and
his boats would bring him down the steps to the boathouse.

"Jesus, Bud, what in Christ's name are you doing here?" he
would shout, bursting through the door. And then in a distraction of
fright he would dash about, securing the lines on the boats and stow-
ing the oars, life preservers, and fishing gear in order to save his treas-
ures from the onslaught. By this time rolls of thunder were
ominously close, and down the lake we could see rain falling in shift-
ing gray curtains. Although it would be fifteen minutes at least before the storm reached us, Oscar became frantic once he had done his
best by his beloved boats.

"Oh, goddamn, Bud, cut the crap and come up to the kitchen. You can watch things better from there."

"Oscar, the storm won't hurt you."

"Oh, Jesus Christ, maybe not, but why take the chance? Come on, Bud, or I'll kick your ass up the steps in front of me."

We would leave the boathouse just as lightning rent the sky overhead and the first rain spattered on the walk in large, pelting drops. Like a mangy dog scrambling out of the water on a rocky beach, Oscar, bent double to shield his face, would all but claw his way up the steps. Gaining the kitchen porch, he would shake his clothes and boots as though a few raindrops had soaked him as thoroughly as a cloudburst. "Goddamn, Bud, you can stay out here if you want, but I'm going inside." And then he would quickly dart in through the screen door.

After the violence of the storm had passed and the thunder was retreating in ever fainter cannonades to the east, the trees dripping and heavy with water, Oscar would join me on the porch, full of jokes and snickers now to cover up his earlier terror.

"Jee-sus, Bud, that was a real bitch. Sounded like a whole herd of elephants up there, pissing to beat hell."

The storm would leave the air clean and cool, with the fresh scent of evergreen coming off the wet trees. With all the bravado of the clown feigning courage after fright, Oscar would saunter down the boathouse steps, pausing on the landing to let go a fart.

"Ah, that feels good! Nothing like a bit of thunder and lightning to clean the gut. Come on, Bud, help me sweep the water out of the boathouse."

ONCE OR TWICE A SUMMER my mother would come up for a week or ten days, traveling overnight on the train from Grand Central Station. Usually she came alone because my father loathed the

Adirondacks. For a brief spell the lives of the four of us—Grandfather, Julia, Oscar, and I—were civilized with order and activity.

Mother loved to walk, and two or three times a week she would have Oscar drop us off at some spot on the lake and force me to straggle behind her while she clipped off three or four miles on dirt roads. Sometimes we visited a deserted camp or walked to Bartlett's Carry at the end of the lake, where there was an ancient earthen dam and a canoe portage to Middle Saranac Lake. When Mother was in residence, we always ate well and promptly; I was in bed by nine-thirty or ten; Oscar was clean shaven and bathed; and Julia, brimming with joy, was delighted that at last someone appreciated her work.

"Oh, Mrs. Spence," she would say, "thank the Lord you're here. Now, Mr. Dunlap, if you don't mind my saying so, has no idea how to run a proper house. Take that stove of mine. Don't you think . . ." Before she could finish, Mother would cut her off. "Yes, yes, I know, Julia, cooking with that coal stove is difficult. But you have to realize that up here in the Adirondacks we can't have all the luxuries of life near New York."

But best of all, when Mother came, there were other faces to be seen and other places to go. We had friends on the lake to dinner, went to evening movies at the inn, had picnics at various islands and points down the lake. Much of this activity was lily-picking nonsense to Grandfather, who was not eager to share hot dogs and hamburgers with blackflies and ants. (In his defense, getting in and out of small boats with his game leg were feats of agility he was not about to attempt.) As for movies, surely he knew of them, but like a computer to an octogenarian today, they were merely a frivolous distraction.

In all these activities Oscar was no more than ferryman. Dreading the lake at night, when we went to the movies, and equally frightened of venturing into unknown waters by day, he lapsed into servile complaint and ill temper. Informed by Mother that she was planning a picnic the next day on Buck Island, at the head of Saginaw Bay, Oscar was all sweet compliance: "Yes, Mrs. Spence, I'll be glad to get everything ready. You just tell me what you want, and I'll have it in the boat for you." But the following day, carrying the picnic baskets, wood for the fire, blankets and towels to the boathouse, he was Shakespeare's Bartolph.

"Shit, what does anyone want to go on a picnic for when you can eat twice as good at home?" he'd whine. "Goddamn, the bugs will eat us alive."

Mother's favorite picnic ground was on Fish Creek, at the end of which today lies a vast public campground. Here a chain of ponds empties through the creek into Upper Saranac Lake. It took some forty-five minutes to get there by boat, starting down toward the Narrows, then just short of them turning north up a long bay to the swampy entrance to the creek.

Once within the creek, the landscape in those days was utterly wild. There was a flat, windless expanse of swamp that cut a swathe forty yards wide through the bordering forest. Lily pads and marsh grass choked the narrow, slow-moving stream with such a growth of vegetation that in the heat of July it had an aura of Africa. The creek itself was no more than a quarter of a mile long, but because it backtracked on itself time and again, it seemed to be twice that length. Its passage was so obstructed with submerged logs and stumps that for stretches it was safer to pole the boat with oars than to risk the propeller.

In this wind-sheltered environment masses of bugs hovered above the water, and bullfrogs slapped their bodies into the stream with metric regularity. Often in rounding a turn we would surprise a flock of ducks, which would explode from the marsh grass and take off in a clatter of wings and cacophony of quacks that set the swamp alive with sound. (Fish Creek, I might add, is unrecognizable today as the same place where we had our picnics. Following World War II,

George Donaldson—forever pyramiding his grubstake of Grandfather's truck and $10,000—bought the land surrounding the creek and on a ninety-nine-year lease subdivided it into tiny lots, each with a cottage hardly bigger than a chicken coop. Next door to the public campground George opened a general store selling everything from fishing worms to canned ham. All summer the store is so jammed you nearly need a respirator to breathe.)

Every picnic was an exhilarating break in the daily routine and an escape, if only for a few hours, from the at times stifling isolation of Woodwil. Preparations began at 9:30 A.M., as Mother consulted with Julia in the kitchen, then rooted in the linen closet for towels and old blankets to sit on. Soon after 11:00 the guests would begin to arrive by boat from other camps on the lake, and by 11:30 the urgent question was whether at that indecent hour it was sinful to have a drink at Woodwil before leaving.

I whined and nagged to be allowed to leave with the provisions in the tin boat well in advance of the rest of the party, who went in the outboard with Oscar. This timing of departures was critical because without a generous head start I would be left behind, and the adults would arrive at the picnic ground with not even a beer for solace. Needless to say, the adults' dithering between sin and temperance, coupled with Oscar's foot-dragging reluctance to in carry things down to the boathouse, meant that I would be hardly half a mile down the lake before they roared by in the outboard, waving merrily as I thumped along.

Part of the pleasure of a picnic no doubt lies in the discomfort of sitting on rock, balancing a soggy paper plate in your lap, and savoring the ashen taste of charred hot dogs. Oscar was certainly right: you eat much better at home. But picnics offer the irresistible lure of the primitive, the sense of being close to the elemental. Some people, of course, make a regular fête champêtre of a picnic, with sandwiches of smoked Virginia ham, artichoke hearts, potted shrimp, pâté, and wine, all packed in a fancy wicker basket. Mother's picnics, however, were on the spartan side. The potato salad was Julia's best, but there were never quite enough hot dogs to go around, and slicing the tomatoes with someone's pocket knife (the kitchen paring knife had inadvertently been left behind) made a mess of the sandwiches. Also, dessert was only marshmallows toasted over the fire and donuts for the coffee.

But food and drink were only part of the ritual. First, everyone swam off the rocks, and then, sitting in the sun to dry, the adults were full of reminiscences of twenty and thirty years earlier, of a day just like this one, with a company of teenage girls and boys. After lunch one person was sure to try his luck fishing, another to take, or at least to pretend to take, a nap, a third to persuade me, as the only child along, to explore a bit back in the forest. Oscar in the meantime was forever fretting about the boats, lest the wake of a passing outboard would punch a hole in one of ours or the lines would mysteriously come loose and the boats would drift away. Finally, just as in departing from Woodwil, when the remains of the picnic were packed up, the adults in the outboard would leave me far behind because pride would not allow me to give a guest my place in the tin boat.

Still, the trip back through the creek, with the slanting late-afternoon sun burnishing the swamp and flashing off the dark water, was a moment of high adventure. The propeller of the boat rotated so slowly and was cast of such heavy bronze that in most stretches there was no need to shut off the engine for fear of weeds. As the boat pushed its way through, bumping off stumps, plowing through water lilies like an icebreaker through soft spring ice, I had the world to myself. And when I reached the end of the creek, with the open water of the bay beyond, it was with an exaltation of independence that I set the bow toward home.

This way of life, I am sure, gave my mother confidence in my odd existence in keeping a solitary old man company at Woodwil. Her only concern was for the loneliness she knew gnawed at me at times. In those perniciously misplaced gestures of compassion that only a mother is capable of, she would once or twice a summer send up a school acquaintance to be my companion for a week or so. Naturally, the child she selected would not really be my friend but the son of one of her friends, and naturally, too, he and I would get along with the sulky, grudging suspicion of two dogs eating at the same dish. Every boy is fascinated with engines, and for my companion's full stay I would have to surrender the tiller of the tin boat or dream up fanciful excuses, such as vapors in the gas line, for why we could not go out at all. He would want to fish when I wanted to swim, target shoot when I wanted to go out in the woods.

Only one visit I remember as a success. That was when Uncle Boyce, newly taken with the fervor of Christian Science under the tutelage of his fiancé, came up to stay at the camp while I was there. Because he had already discarded me as beyond hope of redemption, Boyce in his evangelical zeal perceived an easy convert in my guest, and every morning bullied him into a fishing expedition, figuring the solitude of midlake was a fitting site for proselytizing. As it turned out, the boy, a strange, shy, introverted youth, was not quite the malleable material Boyce had hoped for. But six months later the poor lad had a severe mental breakdown—congenital, I suspect, as he was not the first of his family to suffer such—and was led away shouting that he was Jesus Christ come to save the world.

IN GRANDFATHER'S MIND, mastery of the skills and lore of the water was as much a part of a gentleman's being as the blue blood in his veins. Thus, the one unpardonable blemish on the character of Adirondack natives was that they could not swim. When he learned that my only cousin—his namesake, no less—also could not swim, he took immediate and typically extreme action. He tied a rope, fastened to the end of a short pole, around the unfortunate seven-year-old boy's waist and without a second thought cast him into the lake, shouting, "Now, swim, boy! Swim!"

It was only natural, then, that Grandfather wanted me, the only grandchild worthy of his affection, to learn the arts of the gentleman mariner. I was to be a canoeist, sailor, and oarsman, Adirondack guideboat style. Canoeing came first, and every evening one June, Oscar was instructed to take me out and show me how to wield a paddle. Oscar, unfortunately, was about as adept with a paddle as a bear is with chopsticks. Many a lovely sunlit evening was lost to our eyes as we zigzagged down the bay, alternately splashing each other and cursing the bugs that collected in a whining halo about our heads.

Grandfather's nautical ambitions for me reached their apogee in sailing. In his youth, he claimed, he had been the very devil of a buccaneer at the tiller and sheet. If ever I was to sit around the fantail and exchange yarns with gentlemanly amateur yachtsmen, clearly I would have to learn to sail. The cost and maintenance of a regular sailboat was out of the question in those straitened times, but Grandfather solved the problem with typical Scots ingenuity: he bought a sailing rig for the canoe, with leeboards, rudder, mast, and sail. By heaven, he proclaimed, if I could master a sailing canoe, there wasn't a three-masted schooner afloat that I couldn't take round Cape Horn. In that he wasn't far wrong because the canoe under sail proved so tippy that I became inured to dunkings in the lake.

The most immediate obstacle to getting me under sail lay in fitting the canoe with the sailing rig, which required securing a foot for the mast in the bottom of the canoe and fittings for a rudder at the stern, and installing a new seat in the bow with a hole to hold the mast in place. A moderately proficient handyman could have accomplished these adaptations in an hour or so, but Oscar straight off put a hole in the bottom of the canoe while securing the foot for the mast. The first time I took to the water, one of the fittings for the rudder tore loose—more of Oscar's handiwork. All the same, with patches, multiple curses, and one or two frenzied moments when Oscar threatened to drive his hammer through the side of the canoe if the new front seat wouldn't fit, the boat was made reasonably watertight and seaworthy.

Then came the problem of teaching me to sail. Grandfather's first inspiration was to go out in the canoe with me, until Julia, the one commonsensical person among the four of us, pointed out that the boom wouldn't pass over his head unless he sat on the bottom, so he would be as doomed as a pig in a gunnysack in the event we capsized, as we surely would. Failing this solution, Grandfather decided he would instruct me first on land, with paper and pencil, and then, once I was familiar with the theory, from the cockpit of the Chris-Craft. This was a bit like teaching a person to ski by using fingers and matchsticks on a cake of ice, yet Grandfather had enough of an imperious nature to give courage to a niddering idiot and to command obedience from a recalcitrant donkey.

Under this system, in two weeks or so, with Grandfather bellowing, "Head her up, Bud, head her up!" I learned enough of sailing to go out in a gentle breeze and tack far enough up the bay for a good run before the wind back to the boathouse. Of course, despite all the patching and caulking, the canoe leaked slightly from Oscar's hole in the bottom, and any wind stronger than a sneeze was likely to capsize me. But the joy and independence of running before the wind, with the water bubbling around the rudder, the lateen sail full and straining, were unforgettable.

And then it all ended. As happened every third or fourth time I went out, one afternoon I capsized in the middle of the bay, trusting Oscar to rescue me in the Chris-Craft. In the confusion of pulling me over the side, he allowed the stern of his boat, with the propeller still turning slowly, to swing over the sail floating flat on the water, and in one quick pass both mast and sail were rendered kindling and rags.

"Oh, goddamn, I've done it now!" cried Oscar in one of his more restrained curses.

Two or three years later, in his last summer at Woodwil, while I was out west with my parents, Grandfather had his own climactic moment on the water. With Oscar at the wheel of the Chris-Craft, he was taking two elderly ladies, who had been his guests for tea, back to the inn. Rounding a point about half a mile from Woodwil, they were struck amidships by a teenage cowboy at full throttle in another Chris-Craft. In seconds they were floundering in the water, with the *Arodasi* at the bottom of the lake. Grandfather always declined to go into details of the accident, but Oscar, on the only occasion I remember him to have uttered a word of admiration and praise for the old man, was effusive: "Jesus Christ, Bud, you should have seen your granddaddy. None of us could swim except him, but by Jesus, all alone he rescued all three of us."

Apparently, the miscreant boy did leap into the water to help, but in the main it was Grandfather's reliable breaststroke and those life preservers and kapok flotation cushions that saved the day. "You should have seen him," Oscar told me. "Christ, I never did see him before without that thatch he wears on his head. But I'll be goddamned if, puffing like a bald old walrus, he didn't get us all to shore. You got to hand it to the old bastard; your granddaddy really had it in him when the chips were down."

Grandfather, in the modesty he was occasionally capable of, would not have described his actions in quite that way. But no matter: in the moment of crisis he had been as stout as any of his Scottish heroes, "brave old John Knox" included.

CHAPTER FIVE

THE SARANAC INN, on Upper Saranac Lake, and the Trudeau Sanatorium, twelve miles away in Saranac Lake village, reflected in quite
different yet strangely parallel ways the changing fortunes not only
of their region but of a whole social standard and its way of life. Both
opened within a few years of each other in the late nineteenth century. Seventy years later both closed down, again within a few years
of each other, at almost the midpoint of the twentieth century. Each
was celebrated in its time, the inn as one of the great resort hotels of
the Northeast, the sanatorium as a world-class hospital for the cure
of tuberculosis. Each was a sprawling conglomeration of buildings
nurturing its own individual culture. The inn coddled the affluent,
self-styled WASP elite; the sanatorium was the insulated world of
those with a serious communicable disease.

As a child I thought the inn a kind of magical place where every-
body was dressed in a style of summer finery that is almost impossible to imagine today. Every time Oscar went over there in the
Chris-Craft, I went along with him. Later I went on my own in the
tin boat or the outboard as often as Grandfather would send me.
Sometimes I went to pick up a package that had arrived there for
him, or, failing that, I dreamed up every kind of spurious errand—oil
for the outboard when there was already plenty in the boathouse or
fishing worms when I didn't intend to fish. I just liked to hang around

68

the inn, talking to the college boys and girls who were employed there. And there was always the hope that some guest, for a ten-cent tip, would send me to the general store for a newspaper or magazine.

In Saranac Lake village, however, I was under strict orders not to speak to anyone on the street or go into any shop, drugstore, or market unless an adult was with me. I doubt whether there was much chance of my encountering a tubercular patient and being exposed to infection, but Grandfather had persuaded Mother that no precaution was too great when there was the slightest risk of my falling victim to the dread disease. Thus, in quite radically divergent ways I was made familiar with the different worlds of the inn and the sanatorium, and each left an imprint on my memory that is still vivid today.

The Saranac Inn, located at the extreme northern end of Upper Saranac Lake roughly two miles from Woodwil, commanded perhaps the most magnificent view in the entire Adirondacks. To the southeast, the inn looked across the large bay to the High Peaks —a jumble of mountains, many of which rose above four thousand feet—and to the east, Whiteface loomed almost solitary, just under five thousand feet, its shape a near-perfect cone against the sky. Indeed, to stand on the lawn in front of the inn's wide verandah was to look out on what appeared to be an unspoiled wilderness, with the lake a mirror to the several islands that formed a foreground to the forest on the far shore and to the gradual sweeping rise of the mountains on the horizon. In brilliant sunshine or cloud-darkened rain, the view was so alluring that the eye never tired of picking out another attraction, whether it was a great blue heron flying low over the water or a high wind kicking up whitecaps on the bay. With such a glorious panorama it was no wonder that the inn drew the rich and wellborn from all over the Northeast and as far away as Chicago and Charleston, South Carolina.

Though the inn was originally built in the 1880s and was at first called the Prospect House, it was not until Harrington Mills bought

it, shortly before World War I, that it attained its full splendor as a resort hotel. A hefty man who tipped the scales at well over 250
pounds, Mills's expansiveness equaled his vision for the inn. The
original building had been a large white clapboard structure with a
red, hipped roof that would have suited an outsized barn in Vermont
but on Upper Saranac seemed as appropriate as a glass-walled Manhattan office tower. Mills added a wing to this building, the Annex,
which was about as imaginative as a shoe box and similarly shaped.
But this addition was just the beginning of his building aspirations.
Strung along the lakeshore was a small metropolis of white clapboard guest cottages, and directly in front of the main building Mills
constructed a columned pavilion, the Casino, where games, dances,
and parties were held. Finally, in front of the Casino, an impressive
T-shaped main dock jutted into the lake a good sixty feet.

Sprawlingly laid out, the inn could accommodate between seven
hundred and eight hundred guests. Located some twelve miles from
the nearest town, it had to be as self-sufficient as possible. Relying on
the outside world only for food and those household supplies indispensable to opulent living, the resort had its own power plant, a dairy
and farm three miles away, dormitories for the summer help, a steam
plant for heat and hot water, a general store and fresh vegetable and
meat markets that not only supplied the inn's dining rooms but also
catered to the lake's summer community. And this was not all.
There was a sizable building for the laundry, extensive stables, a separate blacksmith shop, and parking garages. Three miles away, on a
spur line of the New York Central tracks to Montreal, the inn main-
tained its own railroad station. Capping it all was the inn's post office, with a full-time federal postmaster and—until recently, as a last
vestige of bygone glories—its own zip code.

Hardly more than a quarter mile away, Mills laid out a magnificent eighteen-hole golf course so verdant with the plentiful rainfall

as to rival Grandfather's bluegrass region of Kentucky. There were tennis courts, putting greens at the inn proper as well as at the golf club, riding stables, and a whole armada of canoes, guide boats, and splendidly graceful antique launches that—for a fee, naturally—took inn guests on tours of the lake.

For the sporting clientele, there were guides for fishing expeditions, and each Sunday afternoon trap shooting took place off the end of the main dock. Weekly dances and bridge parties were held in the Casino. But even this catalog of diversions omits Mills's most solicitous service to his guests, at least during the Prohibition-parched twenties: a private bootlegger who, on a whispered order, would see to it that a bottle of whiskey or gin was left in a guest's bedroom, along with the fresh linens and towels. (The bootlegger, Major Dawson—and Major really was his name, not a bogus Kentucky title—used to tell the story of some golfers who, alarmed at seeing suspicious-looking men in the woods lining the course, rushed to the inn to urge Mills to call the police. Major, getting wind of the affair, got to Mills in the nick of time, explaining that the men were simply his crew hiding the latest shipment of booze from Canada.)

To mitigate, or perhaps more accurately to atone for, all this ostentatious indulgence, there was (and still is today) within easy walking distance of the inn a charming little "nondenominational" (i.e., Episcopal) church built of logs. Mills had not constructed this church, but it was happily located for guests repenting of a Saturday night's indiscretions.

Like a vast beached cruise ship, the inn required a staff almost as numerous as its guest list. Spread out over acres and acres of landscaped grounds, with intersecting roads and footpaths, the place was alive with employees busily engaged in keeping the paying guests well fed, entertained, and rested. Seldom did I visit there without encountering three or four men in white coveralls toting buckets and brushes or high aloft on ladders scraping and applying the coats of paint that kept these buildings spotlessly white and glaringly out of place in the surrounding forest.

Then there were those college boys and girls who during off-hours used to loll about the "back dock"—the waterborne service entrance to the inn—swimming and sunbathing, the girls in latex bathing suits that sent Oscar into snorting, thigh-slapping seizures of lust. "Jesus Christ, Bud, did you see that blonde? I swear, give me one night with her, and I'd teach those college kids a thing or two. Oh, Lord Almighty, hot diggety-dog, makes me nearly faint just thinking about it." I, just twelve or thirteen, really had no idea what was bothering Oscar, but when he was in this fever of histrionics, smacking the heel of his hand to his forehead, we were often in danger of striking one of the buoys that marked the channel into the back dock or of ramming a canoe paddled by an inn guest.

The inn's general store and meat market employed soda fountain attendants and butchers; in the various workshops and outbuildings there were plumbers and carpenters to repair leaky faucets and squeaky doors, as well as mechanics to service the launches; and on the lakefront there were lifeguards to watch over the children's bathing beach. The caddies at the golf course earned their own keep in fees for carrying two heavy leather bags that would have all but broken the back of a burro, but the golf and tennis pros had only two months in which to make a living wage. (Major Dawson, on the other hand, easily saved enough money to open a popular bar just down the road from the inn in later years.) There is no telling the amount of money local people made selling firewood to the inn, cutting ice on the lake, or shoveling the snow off the roofs. In its 1920s heyday the resort was an engine of employment and profit, and Harrington Mills, his great paunch a fitting symbol of its sybaritic character, presided over the whole enterprise like some mythic panjandrum, his efforts devoted solely to keeping his customers happy and spending freely.

LIKE MANY SNOBBISH WATERING HOLES in its day, the Saranac Inn was restricted: that is, anyone not of or even perceived to be not of good WASP lineage was excluded. In fact, it was not until after World War II, when the Supreme Court struck down "restrictive covenants" and other discriminatory practices, that such a policy was declared illegal, at least for public accommodations such as the inn.

In today's multicultural world it is perhaps difficult to realize the extent of the anti-Semitism and general xenophobia so pervasive among affluent WASPs prior to World War II. The Irish, the Italians, anyone even suspected of a drop of Hispanic blood—all were regarded as "lesser breeds" by a group whose own origins were often only two or three generations removed from Ellis Island. It took Franklin Roosevelt, the "country squire in the White House" who was himself descended from Dutch patroons, to expose the pretensions of this self-anointed elite in his address to the Daughters of the American Revolution in Washington: "Fellow immigrants," he began. It was the Jews, however, who bore the brunt of WASP bigotry and who were singled out not as God's chosen people but as victims in a particularly vicious modern version of bearbaiting.

It is sometimes argued today that in assessing the anti-Semitism of such figures as poet T. S. Eliot, some mitigating consideration should be given to the climate of the times; indeed, prior to the revelations of the Holocaust, good WASP parents schooled their children in mindless bigotry with the same unthinking nonchalance they adopted in spooning cod liver oil into them. Still, the means by which Harrington Mills and others in his position enforced their restriction policies reeked of deliberate cruelty. Not only were Messrs.

Bache, Lewisohn, Kahn, and Seligman, who lived at the southern end of the lake, forbidden to set foot in the inn, but even the golf course was declared off-limits. In one of the resort's strangest arrangements, Jules Bache, who was a Wall Street financier, was allowed to play golf on the inn's course only after Labor Day. As a perverse sort of practical joke one year, Bache played on Labor Day proper, whereupon Mills rushed onto the course wagging his finger and complaining, "Jules, Jules, you're breaking our agreement."

I can remember my father, who agreed to visit Woodwil only on condition that he could play golf, returning outraged from his round: the pro had almost forbidden him to play because his friend and partner had a suspiciously Jewish-sounding name. But the dunce cap for inane bigotry goes to the impeccably socialite grandfather on nearby Upper St. Regis Lake who blackballed his own grandchildren from membership in the local yacht club because their mommy had had the indiscretion to marry a man tainted with a smidge of Jewish blood.

In any event the ethnically cleansed exclusivity of the inn, along with its baubles and toys, made it the central playground of the WASP community at the northern end of Upper Saranac. Just to be close by, many people built their camps chockablock to each other on a small bay near the resort's back dock. The largest landowner in the area at three thousand acres, the resort closed many a profitable deal selling lots to prospective camp owners. In fact, Grandfather bought the property for Woodwil from the inn in a scratchy transaction with Harrington Mills that later, however, blossomed into a beautiful friendship.

To cement the ties of social life and entertainment, the inn made sure it was the center of activity. Each summer during the twenties it held a regatta, with sailing and canoe races, swimming and diving, greased-pole and tilting contests. Topping it all was a Chris-Craft race in which Boyce, Grandfather's eldest son, once took the winner's cup. For years that trophy held a place of honor on the living-room mantel at Woodwil. Even during the thirties, when the depression laid a heavy hand on the gaiety and camaraderie of the summer colony, the inn dining room of a Saturday night was often sprinkled with camp owners, and all summer long the general store and meat market next door were as much gossipy gathering places as the Pump Room in Jane Austen's Bath.

To Grandfather especially, old and restricted by his infirmities, the inn was a mecca of friendship and social life. Dinner with Harrington Mills, with drinks beforehand at his cottage, was a high occasion for us. For me it was a liberation from Grandfather's concern about my bowels because Mills insisted I order whatever I liked from the menu. He was the only man I ever remember, except the Mr. Graham of rummy quarrels, who called Grandfather by his first name, John. A wily innkeeper, he had the wisdom always to agree with everything Grandfather said, whatever the subject. "You've hit the nail right on the head, John. I couldn't agree with you more" was his standard response as he raised his arms from that huge ark of a body in amiable surrender.

Then there was a Mr. Vanderhoff, who, with a pallid, almost mute male companion, every summer took a cottage at the inn for several weeks of fishing. Where Mr. Vanderhoff hailed from, I don't know, but his customary mode of attire made him, I am sure, the last ambulatory throwback to a World War I doughboy: a peaked Baden-Powell Boy Scout hat, jodhpurs, and leather puttees worn above high, laced boots. Mr. Vanderhoff never seemed to be without a fishing rod, and when he wasn't talking about the effectiveness of the various spoons, spinners, and plugs he used, he was prating on about the weather. (But, then, the state of the weather was just another aspect of his luck in fishing.) Occasionally he and Mr. Mute would appear near Woodwil late in the afternoon, slowly trolling in a small outboard, and Grandfather, summoning them with his earsplitting whistle, would invite them in for a drink. Then, for an hour or so, while Mr. Vanderhoff rambled on about the strikes he had had or the fish he had landed, Grandfather, no doubt partially rescued by his deafness, would sit with an attentive look that seemed to me a marvel of courtesy and patience. Of course, after a day in which his most exciting event was the delivery of the mail or another complaint from Julia, the appearance of a wooden Indian might have seemed a happy diversion.

Also I remember a Mr. and Mrs. Marshall, who owned a small camp on the back bay, close by the inn. They were a chubby pair and had an endearing amiability about them. I think Grandfather liked them because they were forever asking his advice: From whom should they buy firewood; what did he think was the best way to stop the chipmunks from invading their larder; was stain or paint a better preservative for wood? On many of these subjects Grandfather was no more an expert than an Eskimo is on refrigerators, but that did not stop him from pontificating on all sorts of Adirondack lore. Unfortunately, the friendship nearly came to an end when it turned out that Mr. Marshall was not so amiable when it came to politics, and a pleasant dinner at Woodwil ended in loud voices and angry exchanges. But leave it to Mother. When she arrived a week or so later, the breach was smoothed over with several conversations between the more sensible women.

For many camp owners, however, social life was defined more by where they came from than by any attachment to the inn. Like many summer resorts infested with the socialites of various major cities, Upper Saranac exerted a strong pull on the Main Line of Philadelphia. Moreover, some families were so intertwined by blood and marriage as to form an almost incestuous web of kinship, clinging together in a round of picnics, hiking expeditions, and canoe trips. But, like Mr. Vanderhoff, there were others so dedicated to fishing or some other wilderness pastime such as mountain climbing or canoeing (in a regimen strict as canonical hours, up at five in the morning to visit spots on the lake known for bass or lake trout) that they had no time for the foofaraw of social life. All the same, most camp owners were, like the guests at the inn, as much taken up with the pleasures of one another's company as with the natural wonders of the Adirondacks.

At Woodwil, well into his eighth decade, Grandfather had to make do for the most part with my meager companionship and with the few more or less congenial souls he sought out at the inn. It was often a lonely and solitary life, and the miracle was the contentment and at times even the happiness we did find in our lives together. If there was anyone who was sorely tested—and only now and then—I think it was Oscar. In the early thirties, when the inn was sometimes as empty of guests as a derelict building in the South Bronx, before we returned to Woodwil from an errand, he and I would frequently stand on the porch of the inn store, licking away at our ice cream cones. Looking over at the deserted parking lot, Oscar would intone in a desolate voice: "Jesus, Bud, this place is going to hell in a bucket. Shit, if it weren't for the bucks, I'd get the hell out of here tomorrow. Why your granddaddy wants to hang on to that goddamned place, I don't know. Christ, if it were mine, I'd put a match to it and forget the whole fucking business."

Though sacrilegious, there was some sanity in his words.

THROUGHOUT THE NINETEENTH CENTURY and well into the twentieth, tuberculosis, or TB, was the scourge that AIDS is today. People from all walks of life, women as well as men, young and old, black and white, died of it in large numbers. At a congress on the disease in Paris in 1905, a German doctor reported that one-third of all the deaths and half of the sickness in Germany were owing to TB. In 1907 in the United States alone—with only half the population, or forty-five million people, surveyed—deaths from tuberculosis to-taled 175,000.

Nor did there at that time seem to be any reliable cure. The causes ascribed to it—overcrowding, poverty, diet—and the treatments recommended—high altitude, rest, cold weather—varied as widely as the remedies for the common cold. Moreover, like AIDS, as a communicable disease TB inspired irrational fear and revulsion, as though it gave off an odor of moral as well as physical corruption.

That Saranac Lake, a rundown, largely inaccessible village populated by loggers, trappers, and rustics, became what was eventually to be a world-renowned haven for TB patients and research, was essentially the work of one man: Dr. Edward L. Trudeau. A promising young New York physician back in the 1870s, Trudeau was diagnosed with tuberculosis and sentenced to an early death by his fellow doctors. Under the shadow of death, this enthusiastic outdoorsman decided he would have one last happy vacation in the Adirondack wilds. Miracle of miracles, after weeks in the pure air and evergreen forests, his condition improved. His disease arrested, and starting from Little Red, the tiny cottage where his first patients, New York shop girls Alice and Mary Hunt, spent the winter of 1877 with heat only from a woodstove, Trudeau set about the long task of creating the huge Trudeau Sanatorium.

The sanatorium proper was a collection of large, dark-wood buildings located at the end of Park Avenue. This complex housed the laboratories, main treatment center, infirmaries, patient cottages, and administrative offices. Many other patients were quartered in innumerable "cure cottages" scattered through the residential sections of town. It was, as indeed it called itself, a "cottage sanatorium," where the staff of the individual cottages and doctors from the sanatorium tended patients, who were thus freed from the oppressive impersonality of a huge institution. Many of the cottages (a number are still standing, converted into apartments or bed-

and-breakfast lodgings) were impressive buildings accommodating twenty or more patients, and each had the requisite open porch, often on the second story, where patients, in beds but bundled up in blankets till not much more than their noses were visible, were arrayed in rows to take full advantage of the brisk winter air.

As Grandfather so emphatically stated, camp owners on Upper Saranac "rigorously and frankly" avoided the hordes of patients at the various sanatoria—just as today, in most summer colonies, little social contact occurs between summer people and local townsfolk. Yet I remember driving around on the back streets of Saranac Lake with Oscar, seeing those porches lined with patients in deck chairs or beds and the isolated small knots of strollers on residential sidewalks. In the central shopping district, along Broadway and Main Street, there was something eerie in the absence of all those people I knew were living just blocks away.

Yet, as I learned from the descriptions of a friend who was both an attending doctor and a patient, life among the multitudes of the afflicted was at once stimulatingly cosmopolitan and at the same time hermetically sealed, a life claustrophobically focused on illness and treatment. Though most patients were Americans, foreigners came as well, including Robert Louis Stevenson and Béla Bartók. Every profession and trade was represented, but all were limited by the enforced indolence of the chronically ill.

To set this description of life in the area on a more trivial, personal plane, if Saranac Lake encapsulated for its TB patients a dream of health and well-being, its irresistible attraction for me was Stark's hardware store. Stark's was a capacious brick building, dark and cavernous inside, with tall ladders on wheels fixed to steel rails that alone gave access to countless wooden drawers and cubbyholes lining the walls from floor to ceiling. Written orders for tools, nails, and what-have-you were inserted in a metal tube and then sent, by the snap of a rope handle, whizzing on wires to remote corners of the ground floor. It didn't matter that I seldom bought anything or had little idea of the purpose of most of the merchandise: Stark's was a world of enchantment.

The closing of the Trudeau and other TB sanatoriums in the Saranac Lake area—with their satellite cottages and cohorts of doctors, nurses, and attendants—was abrupt. For all its horror, modern warfare tends to promote medical advances, from surgical procedures to drugs to rehabilitation protocols. And sure enough, soon after World War II an array of revolutionary new drugs and antibiotics, notably streptomycin and other antituberculosis drugs, produced a safe and proven cure for the dread disease. Not only that, but with an honesty and grace not often found even in the scientific and medical fields, especially where money and people's financial security are concerned, the authorities in charge of the various sanatoriums welcomed the cure and, recognizing their own superfluity, closed their doors.

In the process, of course, the economy of Saranac Lake suffered a decline, evidenced today in vacant lots where buildings once stood and in the generally neglected look of many that remain. All the same, the town bravely survives today as the center of an increasingly booming summer tourist trade.

WHEREAS THE CLOSING of the Trudeau Sanatorium was quick and redeemingly beneficial, the collapse of the Saranac Inn was a sorry tale of slow disintegration. Somehow surviving World War II, the inn soon afterward was pawned off by Mills's heirs to successive hotel chains, each of which tried different marketing strategies to salvage an already foundering ark. One chain went in hot pursuit of any type of convention—doctors, Shriners, lawyers, Elks—that might help meet the payroll for the next two weeks; another tried respectability and the old-world traditions of the grand European hotel.

None of these ploys worked, and as the last hotel chain pulled out in the 1960s, the whole place went up for sale in a series of auctions—the main building for demolition and scrap, the cottages, the islands out in the bay, the golf course, the farm, and whatever land might attract a buyer. For a full decade the fifteen or twenty acres of the immediate inn complex, with its cluster of buildings, garages, and barns, seemed in a perpetual state of decay. In the harsh Adirondack climate, paint peeled off, wood rotted, and foundations collapsed in a year or two. The demolition crews could barely keep up with nature's own destruction. I remember peering through cupped hands into the windows and seeing how the floor of the main corridor heaved and buckled as though struck by an earthquake and how the huge fieldstone fireplaces in the lounge were disintegrating in a rubble of rocks.

And then in the 1970s the fire that in the Adirondacks seems to have an uncanny affinity for bankruptcy and insurance claims took the inn. The fire departments of two counties, Franklin and Essex, answered the alarm, but one look at the blazing behemoth of the inn persuaded them that all the waters of the lake could never save it. With practical foresight they turned their hoses on the walls and roofs of nearby cottages and preserved them. All the ensuing summer, bulldozers and trucks worked to smooth over the great black scar left by the fire, and in subsequent years the ground where the inn once stood has been sown with grass, and outlying buildings (cottages excepted) leveled without a trace. Only a short time ago the owner of one of the largest cottages on the lakeshore decided to move it to the site of the inn, so that now my family and other camp owners look across the broad expanse of the bay to a diminutive white clapboard building as inappropriate in its treeless obtrusiveness as the hipped-roofed leviathan of twenty-five years ago.

Protected by the statute of limitations, I can now confess that I have a few treasured mementos of the inn's early days: four splendid bedroom mirrors of a quality available only in pricey furniture stores, which I pilfered under the nose of the wrecking crews, and a number of imposing four-by-twelve-foot beams, aged a good one hundred years, for which I paid some five dollars apiece and which now serve as the underpinnings of a small A-frame located on one of Grandfather's more desirable building lots.

...randfather John R. Dunlap posing in front of Woodwil. This photograph was sent ...a Christmas card to his architects in 1928, the year the camp was completed. ...urtesy of the Adirondack Collection, Saranac Lake Free Library.

John Robertson Dunlap, courtesy of Olivia Spence, c. 1920.

Lewis Spence, courtesy of Olivia
Spence, c. 1939.

The main lodge at Woodwil, courtesy of the Adirondac
Collection, Saranac Lake Free Library, c. 192.

randfather Dunlap and friends in front of Woodwil's guest cottage, courtesy
the Adirondack Collection, Saranac Lake Free Library, c. 1928.

Left to right: uncle John (Jack)
Dunlap, Lewis Spence (rear),
cousin John Dunlap, and
grandfather John R. Dunlap,
courtesy of the Dunlap family,
c. 1934.

Left to right: Lewis Spence, uncle John (Jack) Dunlap,
cousin John Dunlap, and grandfather John R. Dunlap,
courtesy of the Dunlap family, c. 1932.

Barbara Dunlap, wife of cousin John Dunlap, in front of Woodwil,
courtesy of the Dunlap family, c. 1944.

The main porch at Woodwil with its view of the Narrows on
Upper Saranac Lake, courtesy of the Adirondack Collection,
Saranac Lake Free Library, c. 1930.

Saranac Inn, which lay directly across Upper Saranac Lake from Markham Point, courtesy of the Adirondack Collection, Saranac Lake Free Library, c. 1934.

Left to right: Eugenia Blackmore Logan (grandfather Dunlap's second wife), uncle Jack Dunlap, Jack's wife Lorraine, and grandfather Dunlap on the porch at Woodwil, courtesy of the Dunlap family, c. 1932.

CHAPTER SIX

GRANDFATHER'S STYLE OF LIFE, as I look back on it, seemed the
direct reverse of J. P. Morgan's dictum about yachts: if you have to
ask about the cost, you can't afford one. Though a penny-pincher in
many ways—and by necessity after 1929—Grandfather often spent
lavishly on things he clearly couldn't afford. Certainly the park project was a shining example of this prodigality. But from the start
Woodwil was an unstanchable hemorrhage on his dwindling resources.

As originally planned, the camp was to be a reasonably modest
summer place where Grandfather and Isadora could maintain a
household reflecting the social standing of a successful retired businessman. But from the initial drawings, in a conspiracy eagerly abetted by the architect William Distin, who made a reputation as a
designer of Adirondack Great Camps, Woodwil took on a life of its
own. Take the "guidehouse," for instance. By tradition an Adirondack guidehouse was to be just that: a simple dwelling where the
camp guide and his family might live in spartan comfort. But no
sooner did Distin put pencil to paper than Woodwil's guidehouse
evolved into a fully insulated four-bedroom structure with its own
living room, dining room, and kitchen. So comfortable was it, in fact,
that Grandfather decided to keep it as a winter lodge for sons Jack
and Boyce when they came north to hunt deer in the fall, and the ser-

vants' quarters were shifted to a wing added onto the main lodge. In reality, the two men and their friends rarely hunted more than a week every year—and that was in the best of times. Considering that Grandfather and Jack were barely on speaking terms, and that Boyce was in the early throes of Christian Science, which apparently forbade hunting in all forms, the need for such a lodge was negligible. After the 1929 crash there was no money for the large staff of servants Grandfather had contemplated. Thus, Julia and Oscar took up residence in the commodious quarters of the guidehouse, and the servants' wing lay unoccupied.

Then there were the "bachelors' quarters." At the time, Woodwil already had seven double bedrooms—three spacious ones with attached baths in the main lodge, and four in the guidehouse—not including those in the unoccupied servants' wing. It was clearly not a lack of space that required an extra structure. I suspect Grandfather simply was taken with the idea of an additional building with the elegant name *bachelors' quarters*, a throwback to those mythic days in the Kentucky bluegrass region when young bucks came a-courting those fetching Dunlap belles. Granted, the bachelors' quarters, perched on a wooded knoll above the main lodge, were not extravagant, consisting only of a large double bedroom with attached bath. Still, to the best of my knowledge this structure was occupied only once. To confirm how parents' plans go awry, one summer my mother sent up not one but two school chums to keep me company. These boys, much preferring each other's company to mine, decided on arrival that they would stay in the bachelors' quarters, where they holed up each day reading pulp magazines. On the other hand, the place did have a shower, which I used whenever Julia checked the calendar and found I hadn't bathed in two weeks or more.

It was the boathouse, however, that tore a gaping rent in Grandfather's purse. Each spring, when he descended from the train at the Saranac Inn station, Grandfather would insist that Oscar take him on a short inspection trip around the bay to survey the damage ice had done to various boathouses. Nothing seemed to warm his heart more than the sight of splintered decking at the Colgate camp or broken doors on the Bedfords' boat slips. He was obviously seeking solace in company because, invariably, when he reached Woodwil, he was greeted with the sorry spectacle of one or more of the heavy timber-and-rock cradles of his own boathouse either smashed or badly damaged. The boathouse faced a five-mile stretch of open water and was only partially protected by the hook of rock Oscar had such trouble navigating in his landings. Consequently, a brisk west wind during breakup forced tons of ice in a solid phalanx against our puny, man-made structure. With the inevitability of death and taxes, days of work were required to repair the damage. Grandfather's only consolation in those depression days were the pauperish wages of the men doing the work.

Besides work on the boathouse, roofs had to be repaired, new boards laid in wooden walkways where old ones had rotted out, steps replaced, and porch railings rebuilt. Thanks to this continual maintenance, I became as familiar with two-by-eights and number 16 nails as a carpenter's apprentice. George Donaldson and his crew did most of the work because Oscar was competent only to stain the walks between buildings and to retack the bark on those expensive timbers that lent Woodwil its authentically bogus rusticity. Thus, a good part of June each year rang with the sound of hammers and the pleasantly rhythmic stroke of saws. Grandfather, I am sure, lived in a constant state of anxiety over the cost, and there were times when he fell morosely silent. Keeping to his bedroom for a large part of the day, he would occasionally limp down the wooden walks to talk with George and then, cane against hip, stand glumly watching the men at work. A thoroughgoing Victorian who believed in growth and progress, Grandfather found little joy in repair and rehabilitation. Figuratively speaking, he himself was rather patched together, and the incessant maintenance at Woodwil was a reminder that he too might become unstuck at any time.

EVEN ON BRIGHT, sunny days we lived to a large extent in a brown and gray world at Woodwil—dark-stained buildings, the forest, the ground underfoot either rock or duff. On windy days the steely surface of the lake, with gusts blowing up through the Narrows, took on the menacing look of the ocean in a heavy sea. Under a low, rainy sky all one could see of the mountains was a gloomy distant ridge, the peaks shrouded in gray drifts of weeping clouds.

Sensitive to this oppressive monotone, Mother decided to bring color to our lives. Despite the obstacles of soil and weather, she decreed we would have a lawn and flower garden, gay with boxes of geraniums and petunias, along the wooden walks. All servile compliance in Mother's presence, Oscar did the work of creating and tending to these floriferous adornments, but once out of her sight, a string of obscenities accompanied each task: "Goddamn, shit, and hell, what's your mom want? A fucking Garden of Eden out here in the goddamned wilderness?"

The lawn was to be planted in a stretch of more or less level ground, some sixty feet long by thirty wide, along the lakeshore between the boathouse and the guidehouse. The flower garden presented a more perplexing problem because to be properly appreciated from the main lodge it would have to be built as a raised bed against a retaining wall on a bare rock face just below the verandah. For a reasonably capable handyman these projects would have required no more than a week or ten days' work, especially considering that George was to bring in the topsoil and help spread it about. But for Oscar the job was formidable.

Other than rough grading, the principal chore in creating the lawn was to remove a fair-size birch that Mother felt was too large for such a small area. In its place would go two or three birch saplings that would take years to reach maturity. George made quick work of taking down the birch, but the stump and root were Oscar's Augean task. For a good five days he labored with ax, shovel, and crowbar. When he finally finished the job, the mangled roots were strewn about the proposed lawn, and the hole looked like a pit excavated by an army of marauding groundhogs.

Yet once George's topsoil was spread and raked, the grass seed planted, and the first shoots of pale green appeared, Oscar was transformed. With his realization that the lawn was actually going to grow came an impetuous zeal for nurture. The sun barely had time to dry the dew before he was out with a hose, watering. When the grass reached a good four inches and Mother suggested it was time for a first mowing, Oscar was stricken.

"But, Mrs. Spence," he wailed, "if I mow it now, it'll kill it. Can't we wait a week or two?"

"Nonsense, Oscar. Grass is much tougher than you think. Go ahead, it won't hurt it."

Unconvinced, Oscar squatted down and brushed his hand through the delicate shoots as lovingly as a father might stroke the fuzz on a baby's head. "All right," he said. "If you say so, I'll mow it"—wanting to add, I am sure, that, Jesus Christ, he'd kick her ass if it died. After its mowing, the grass looked as beaten and wilted as a dying guppy, but it soon revived.

Thereafter, Oscar was not to be found for a single unscheduled chore but that he didn't have to be summoned from tending his lawn. For the first summer it flourished, and even Grandfather, to whom the idea of a lawn in the Adirondacks had originally been poppycock, was persuaded. In subsequent summers Oscar's heart, predictably, went out of the task, and then the problem was to summon him to the scheduled task of mowing. All the same, a trace of his original zeal remained, and on many a summer evening after dinner he and

Julia could be found sitting quietly on the lawn in deck chairs, admiring the last brilliant colors of the fading daylight.

As might be expected, building the retaining wall for the raised flower bed was a Sisyphean labor for Oscar. In the Adirondacks, rocks in the flat plinth shape that make the stone walls of New England so attractive simply aren't to be found. Instead, they come in lovely erotic shapes that make building almost as difficult as marriage. In no time Oscar found handling them twice as infuriating as Julia in her most reproving mood. He and I collected the first batch of boulders along the lakeshore, going out in the tin boat and combing the beaches and points for any rock that could be pried loose. After three or four mornings of toting them up the long steps from the boathouse to the garden site, we had enough rocks, Oscar was convinced, to build Grand Central Station. Only with the hauling done did he discover that the beautifully rounded stones would not stack one on top of another the way they were supposed to. No sooner would he get three or four heaped together than the fifth would send the whole batch bouncing in disorder down the incline toward the boathouse.

"Mrs. Spence, you can't build a wall with these rocks, no matter what you think," he wailed, blowing out his cheeks to suppress his fury and cursing.

With the ruthless practicality of a Dunlap, Mother suggested a sledgehammer to break up some of the rocks, which might then be used as wedges to hold the boulders in place. For a day, in heavy gloves and safety glasses, Oscar wielded a sledgehammer, smashing rocks as Mother had instructed. In the end, of course, it was George and his crew who completed the job, clearing away the boulders Oscar and I had collected and bringing in a truckload of flat, Vermont-type rocks from some mysterious source. The retaining wall was built and mortared within two or three days and, after being filled with soil, made a gay and colorful bed for the petunias and geraniums. Understandably, Oscar took no interest in the flowers, either in the raised bed or in the window boxes and planters he had filled and positioned to Mother's satisfaction. "Fucking women's work," he called it. In Mother's absence, tending the flowers was left to Julia, who, to Grandfather's approval, brought in sprays to decorate the dining table and his desk in front of the picture window.

WITH THESE CONTINUAL ROUNDS of construction and repair, I too was taken early on with a fever for building. My first project was a pine-bough hut that, wonder of wonders, Oscar helped me build out in the woods. The hut was small, not more than six feet wide, six feet long, and some five feet tall, but it was ingeniously constructed, its walls and roof fashioned by weaving pine, hemlock, and balsam boughs in a lattice framework nailed to four corner posts. We did have a problem getting the posts to stand upright because the duff of the forest floor held them about as firmly as a feather pillow. But once the lattice was nailed on and woven with the evergreen boughs, it was a sturdy structure redolent with the smell of the forest. Sheltered by surrounding trees, it was even fairly weatherproof; my greatest pleasure on a rainy day was to retreat to my hut and gaze out at the silent, dripping forest, imagining myself Huck Finn or some other adventuring character.

The disappointment of the pine-bough hut was, of course, that the following spring I found nothing but a bare skeleton of dead, needleless branches interwoven in the brittle lattice. With a little gumption I could easily have stripped these dry remnants and replaced them, but thirteen-year-old boys are not given to pumping up deflated dreams. Besides, I was taken with a new and far bolder enterprise: the construction of a raft on which, à la Huck Finn, I would float down the Mississippi—aka, the mile-long arm of Saginaw Bay.

My dream of a raft suitable for this voyage called for a vessel that owed more to Jules Verne than to Mark Twain. I wanted something that would accommodate a fair-size tent, a hearth, and such lesser luxuries as a comfortable cot. I would also need sufficient cold storage—Oscar would get me the ice—for several days' supply of soda pop, the fish I was sure to catch, and the hot dogs I could eat when I got tired of perch and bullheads (the Adirondack name for catfish). With these specifics in mind I spent several days with graph paper and pencil, sketching various designs that I would then submit to Oscar for appraisal. Like all lowbrow philistines, Oscar was woefully unappreciative: "What the hell do you think you've got there? Christ, you couldn't build that fucking thing in a month of Sundays. Use your head, Bud. The barge is just what you want."

The barge! Had he told me to build my raft out of a toilet seat, I could not have been more put out. The barge was thick with coal dust, and moreover, it was so heavy and ungainly it would have taken me several days just to get it around the point and out into open water.

The upshot was that, like all visionaries, I would have to do it myself. Down the shoreline, several hundred yards from Woodwil and out of sight of Oscar and other nonbelievers, I began my solitary task. My plan was to nail a number of logs together with long two-by-eight-inch crosspieces. Then, having successfully constructed the framework of the raft, I would somehow—this I had not really worked out—lash four oil drums to the underside for flotation.

A simple project, as any intelligent person could see. But I was a dummy. To begin with, I wasn't strong enough to cut down and then get into the water logs big enough to make a suitable raft. The logs got smaller and smaller until they were barely more than outsize saplings. Next, nailing them together with the two-by-eights while standing waist deep in water was like catching eels with one's bare hands. The logs bounced and hopped about, and no sooner had I nailed one to another than the third broke loose. Sure enough, Oscar, hearing the sound of hammering, appeared on the bank above me.

"What you doing there, Bud?" He knew full well what I was doing, but to squeeze the greatest enjoyment from my despair he went on, "Looks like you're trying to nail some poles together. Some kind of fish weir?"

Had I tried to speak I would surely have burst into tears. Seeing my pitiable expression, Oscar relented and broke out with his good news.

"If you're still thinking of building a raft, Bud, I think I got just the thing for you. Saw it floating out in the lake from the boathouse about an hour ago and pulled it in with the tin boat. It's a big old barn door or something. But I think I can help you tie on some empty gas cans and it'll float just fine. Jesus, it'd be a hell of a lot better than anything you could build."

There was a side of Oscar, gentle and thoughtful in his sly, deceitful way, that now and then made him lovable. The barn door was indeed an almost perfect fulfillment of my Huck Finn dream: some ten feet square, it sat a good ten inches above the water with me aboard once it was rigged with the gasoline cans Oscar lashed on with heavy wire. I had no tent to pitch, but a tarpaulin slung over a rope made an acceptable substitute. A hearth for an open fire was clearly out of the question, but a sterno stove would be perfect for frying the few perch I caught. In shallow water, with a pole, I could navigate the raft with some dexterity, but Grandfather had no trouble dissuading me from venturing farther than a few hundred yards out into the lake. Although I never made my voyage down Saginaw Bay, on windless, sunny days as I poled along the shoreline to peer into the deep caverns made by toppled trees or rounded the point at the end of Woodwil's peninsula to explore the coves and rock faces of the cliffs there, I could indeed make the imaginative leap to the Mississippi.

·   ·   ·

HIS HYPERBOLE NOTWITHSTANDING, Grandfather was not far
off the mark when he said that Woodwil had all the comforts of a
Newport villa. To be sure, there were no lavish parties, tennis courts,
or minions hurrying hither and yon. For all its appointments, Woodwil was no Vanderbilt Breakers, but with Julia and Oscar to attend to
us, the luxuries of the Chris-Craft, the woodland park, and the expansive panorama of the lake and mountains, we lacked for little.
Moreover, with a bedroom and bath to myself, being seen to bed and
wakened in the morning by Julia, clothes and linens changed and
washed, teeth and bowels checked every day, I was as indulged as any
spoiled Newport stripling.

It was no doubt his concern for the corrupting influence of this
coddling that prompted Grandfather each spring to pronounce that
we would build a "rough camp." There, I would experience the simple, healthy outdoor life of a true Adirondack woodsman, stripped of
the diversions of the idle rich. Furthermore, the rough camp would
be located on Black Pond, deep in the trackless wilderness of the infamous Black Pond Swamp, at the foot of Boot Bay Mountain, some
two miles southeast of Woodwil.

Now, in my child's imagination there was something almost
mythic about both a rough camp and Black Pond. To begin with, a
rough camp, as Grandfather described it, was not merely a spot
where one spent a night or two in a pup tent, cooked over an open
fire, and after a hasty cleanup moved on to the next campsite. Rather,
it was a semicivilized camping spot with one or more wooden tent
platforms, a boulder fireplace equipped with an iron grill, a couple of
outdoor tables, and a privy at a discreet remove from the living area.
Most important, such a camp featured several securely anchored,
weatherproof boxes to store the tents, sleeping bags, cooking equipment, tinned goods, and staples essential to comfortable woodsy living. In a word, it was a place to which a camper in search of intimate

yet not too rugged communion with nature might return year after year for an extended stay of fishing and hiking or just silent contemplation. Which philosopher, other than Oscar, might share this rustic fastness with me, Grandfather never specified.

If the idea of the rough camp held me in its thrall, perhaps even more magical was its proposed location on Black Pond. In the 1930s, despite the opulent homes built by the Du Ponts, the Lewisohns, and the like, the Adirondacks possessed vast tracts of unspoiled wilderness. In the region surrounding Upper Saranac and its adjoining lakes and ponds, no area was regarded as wilder than Black Pond and its encircling swamp. No less an authority than George Donaldson talked of three or four men who within recent memory had disappeared while deer hunting there, never to be seen again. During Woodwil's construction a team of horses brought over by barge to haul heavy timbers broke out one night and, like the hunters, disappeared, untraceable, in the swamp.

If the bogs and fallen trees, the dense forest cover, the tall marsh grasses, and alder thickets were not enough to confuse even the most experienced woodsman, there were also said to be numerous patches of quicksand to swallow up the lost and panicked wanderer. Hidden away in pristine isolation, the pond itself was sure to be a spawning site for trout, its shores frequented by mink and otter, bear, raccoon, fox, and coyote.

But to this heady vision of a wilderness paradise there was one stubborn obstacle: How exactly might one find a way into Black Pond, let alone build a rough camp there? Theoretically, there were two ways of reaching the pond: one, by means of a supposedly blazed trail leading in from the foot of Saginaw Bay; the other, by water, up Black Pond Creek. This narrow tributary meandered for some three miles through the desolate swamp before emptying into Upper Saranac at the eastern end of the large bay on which the Saranac Inn fronted.

Clearly, the more direct route was overland via the blazed trail. On Grandfather's word that the state conservation department had assured him the trail did exist, Oscar and I set off late one July morning to discover the hidden splendors of Black Pond. As befit such a daring undertaking, we departed in the outboard outfitted with a backpack for a picnic lunch, a compass on which Oscar knew only how to locate magnetic north, and my Winchester .22. Oscar carried an ancient .30–.30, the stock of which was notched and carved to record the innumerable deer Boyce and Jack had slain in their youth. The guns were mandatory. Though edgy about the rumored quicksand, Oscar was all but traumatized by the thought of bear and bobcat.

We set off down the lake with Oscar in the bow singing in a show of bravado, "Where do we go from here, boys, where do we go from here?" But as explorers we were sadly lacking in the grit and determination Lewis and Clark had shown. Once ashore at the foot of Saginaw Bay we blundered about in the woods for a good hour and a half without sighting a single blaze. Granted, we never ventured more than a hundred yards into the forest because Oscar refused to lose sight of the lake for more than five minutes. Our lunch, taken sitting on a log by the shore, was a dolorous occasion. Still, in packing up, Oscar was not one to admit failure without a show of defiance: he got off a single, explosive shot with the .30–.30, aimed in the general direction of that fucking Black Pond.

Grandfather was comfortingly reassuring. The trail had been a stupid idea. Even if it did exist, we would never be able to get a canoe in through the forest, let alone the materials for the tent platforms, outdoor tables, and privy. The answer was for George Donaldson to cut a navigable passage through Black Pond Creek. I would go along to handle the canoe.

When I say that on a map the creek is three miles long, I speak only a factual truth. In my mind it was a hundred miles long, winding through such a hemmed-in, viewless swamp as to disillusion even Humphrey Bogart and his African Queen. When George and I had made our way perhaps a third of a mile up the stretch of creek that was cleared, we were met by a veritable portcullis of fallen trees and snags blocking our way. George was equipped with a double-bladed ax and a timber hook. I don't exaggerate when I say that with ten blows he could cut through a log as big around as a man's thigh. But no sooner had he cut through one fallen trunk and wrestled it aside with the hook than he would find another equally large or larger tree ten or fifteen feet beyond.

Out on the lake it was a delightful warm summer day, but in the swamp it was stifling, with a windless heat that seemed to press in on the marsh grass and forest beyond. No matter how searing the heat, no native Adirondacker, at least in those days, would think of taking off his shirt, and George worked with his collar buttoned to his throat, in heavy trousers and boots, until his clothing was wringing wet with sweat. I presume he was always looking for a bend in the creek where the forest would open up and we would have before us a prospect of the sluggish stream flowing clear and free. But the view around each bend was always the same: the wide, breathless swamp studded with the bare poles of dead trees, more logs and stumps blocking the creek, and on each side the dark forest, walling in the desolate landscape.

With his immense strength George had enough energy to work for hours without rest, and the sun was low when he called it a day and we headed back to the lake. We had cleared at most half a mile, and it was obvious to anyone but a child that ours was a futile undertaking. Still, during the entire way back, paddling down the creek, hitching the canoe to the outboard where we had moored it, and making for Woodwil across the lake, George, either in his natural wordlessness or in sympathy, never said a word of this to me. Only back at the camp did he tersely sum up to Grandfather the impossibility of reaching Black Pond by the creek. "It's no go, Mr. Dunlap," he reported. "It'd take me a year to clear that creek, and then I'm not sure I'd reach the pond."

In retrospect, my disappointment lay more in failing to see the pond, with its reputedly teeming wildlife, than in the lost chance to create a rough camp. Indeed, the prospect of sleeping out in such a benighted wilderness, far from Grandfather and Julia, was more daunting than my adolescent courage could face. And so with Oscar's help I built what might be called a smooth camp—a tent, a pine-bough bed, and a boulder fireplace—safely close to home, on the point below Woodwil, where I could build an open fire in the evening and, if he wasn't playing cards with Julia, persuade Oscar to take me trolling for pike in the guideboat. It was not the life of a true Adirondack woodsman, but in the gathering dusk, with the wind fallen and the lake as flat and still as sheet steel, I could at least imagine we were on Black Pond.

IT WAS A FULL FORTY YEARS before I actually laid eyes on Black Pond. In the company of a friend who was far more of a woodsman than I, we trekked in with two visiting boys on a trail we blazed from the base of Big Square Bay. The walk in was a delight; we were on high ground, away from the swamp, and hiked largely through a climax forest of towering hemlock and hardwoods as clear of undergrowth as those European forests that are picked clean of every stick of usable wood. We went but a mile and a half, and as we neared the pond, the ground rose along a ridge at the foot of Boot Bay Mountain. Throughout the walk I looked for signs of other hikers, but the forest seemed as untouched by humans as my childhood imaginings had made it. The silence, except for the tramp of our feet, was magical.

And then at last there was the pond: first a silvery glint of water through the trees, then a wider streak, and finally from the bank a full view of the open water. After so many years of being the object of a childhood fantasy, the pond was bound to be anticlimactic. It formed an almost perfect circle some two hundred yards in diameter, swampy along the shore, with broken trees and decaying stumps making access difficult. Here too we found no sign that hikers had preceded us, and certainly there had been no campers, at least in recent years. The pond, to be sure, was pristine and wild, but it seemed an unlikely habitat for the wildlife Grandfather had been confident was there. In fact, with its low, wet shoreline from which no promontory or rock ledge jutted out into the water, it seemed a poor place for a rough camp, despite its remote wilderness setting.

CHAPTER SEVEN

LIKE THEODORE ROOSEVELT, Grandfather professed to be a dedicated conservationist. In praising the glories of the Adirondack Forest Preserve, he wrote: "Under enlightened game laws, with heavy penalties for their violation, game is now steadily multiplying. Ruffed grouse are plentiful, and the deer are increasing rapidly in numbers." But Grandfather's actions belied his earnest prose. Game laws, he decreed, were only for lily pickers and "Mussolinis" (that is, all persons not of Anglo-Saxon stock, whether they were of Italian, Polish, or even Icelandic extraction). Gentlemen of a lineage similar to his were allowed to fish and hunt whenever and whatever they pleased, in season or out. Never, for example, did anyone at Woodwil procure a fishing license. In the cool lake waters of June I was always encouraged to fish for bass, never mind that it was out of season.

In keeping with this sporting tradition, Woodwil could claim a fair arsenal of firearms: the ancient .30–.30, a handsome .303 British rifle that son Jack had been given for moose hunting in Canada, several shotguns from Grandfather's bird-shooting days, my Winchester pump-action .22, and a brace of .38-caliber revolvers that belonged to Boyce. Grandfather himself spurned rifle shooting; clearly a shotgun was the only fitting weapon for an English-style gentleman.

Given this arsenal and Grandfather's sporting views, it was no wonder that I was possessed early on with a bloodlust for hunting. My first weapon was a BB gun, my first prey the birds around camp. A stand of tall birches near the powerhouse was a favorite nesting place for a wide variety of birds, and here the first summer of my stay at Woodwil I wreaked a pretty carnage among the warblers, finches, woodpeckers, and sparrows. In fairness to Grandfather, he never realized the extent of my slaughter of birds at Woodwil. Trusting to the inaccuracy of a BB gun and to my inept marksmanship, he undoubtedly reckoned my killing at five or six birds a summer. Furthermore, Grandfather looked on shooting not only as a sport but as a means for putting game on the table, so it was not long before he urged me to set my sights on red squirrels. Back in his Kentucky youth, he said, there had been no finer delicacy than a freshly killed squirrel pot pie. He was not far wrong. If one can tolerate the pathos of picking apart the carcass of a small squirrel, one can enjoy a dish with the tenderness of young chicken spiced with gaminess to give it distinction.

The critical question, however, was not whether the squirrels could be shot, but whether Julia would cook them. And on this point, she balked.

"You want me to cook a squirrel, Mr. Dunlap?" she asked with eyes as large, pale, and frosty as a Nordic winter moon. "That—and I repeat, that—I will not do."

"But Julia, you've said you've cooked rabbit. I don't see the difference—they're both good, clean, wild animals."

"Mr. Dunlap, where I come from, civilized people eat rabbit; they don't eat squirrels."

"Julia, may I remind you that as a boy, I ate squirrel."

"That's all very well, Mr. Dunlap. What you ate as a boy, you ate as a boy, and I am not quarreling with that. All I say is that I won't eat squirrel. They are dirty little beasts."

"But, Julia, I am not asking you to eat a squirrel. All that Bud and I are asking is that you cook a squirrel. Is that clear?"

"It's perfectly clear, Mr. Dunlap. You don't have to condescend to me. It's simply that I won't either cook or eat a squirrel."

For a moment it looked as though there would be no squirrel pot pie at Woodwil. Then grandfather hit on a compromise. As huntsman, I would not only shoot the squirrels, but also skin and eviscerate them, wash them, and under Julia's direction even place them in the casserole for cooking. In fact, Julia wouldn't even have to serve the squirrels, but merely place the casserole on the table and let Grandfather proceed with ladling them out on our plates. From then on we had squirrel pot pie aplenty, and Julia even lost some of her squeamishness, actually dropping the quartered squirrels into the casserole herself. It took at least four squirrels to make a pie that would feed Grandfather and me, and had not my joy in carnage so thinned the local population, we might have had squirrel four or five times a week.

The trick in squirrel hunting was to find a log or stump in the forest and then, with the fortitude of a yogi, sit as still as a statue, letting the bugs gluttonously feed on me. Within a half hour or so, a squirrel usually gave away its presence. I have never learned a naturalist's way in the forest; the thirst for killing blocked out the aesthetic pleasure of recognizing a rare fungus or identifying a lady's slipper or a fern. But from spending hours on a stump I know the faint whistle of wind in pine needles, the creak of heat in the forest, and, most of all, that insidious, solitary whine of a mosquito circling for my blood.

Over time I actually developed a deep empathy for squirrels. A red squirrel is an irredeemably nasty little brute, by instinct untamable. But a furry, peanut-eating Central Park-type gray squirrel, Grandfather conceded when I discussed the matter with him, was a feasible alternative as a pet. On my thirteenth birthday Grandfather presented me with a caged gray squirrel, complete with trapeze and

exercise wheel to keep the little treasure in shape. Initially the squirrel was a source of joy and infinite jest, but the idea of caging an animal was morally repugnant to my mother. While I was off at school,
she would let it loose to dash about my room, upsetting my carefully
arranged lead soldiers and leaving stains and quaint little droppings
on my bed pillow. How delicious it was, though, after capturing my
pet atop the curtains or perched on the windowsill, to cuddle the
sweet creature or watch it nibble its diet of seeds. On several occasions the squirrel escaped into the house at large. One afternoon, to
my mother's hilarity, it disrupted a bridge party; when the ladies saw
the squirrel bounding about the living room, they actually did get up
on their chairs and scream.

Then I caught a cold that deepened, sinking into my chest and
bronchial tubes. I began to wheeze and gasp for breath, and Mother,
fearing pneumonia or pleurisy, called the doctor. He diagnosed
asthma, caused by the fur of the squirrel, whose cage sat next to my
bed. There was no choice but to get rid of my dear pet. Perhaps in
atonement for the gift and certainly in an act of great kindness,
Grandfather had one of the squirrels I had shot stuffed and mounted
by a taxidermist—clearly the most modest commission the man had
ever completed. Thereafter my squirrel held an honored place atop
the bookcase at Woodwil, just above the remaindered copies of
Grandfather's Jefferson biography.

FOR ALL THEIR EARLY ASSOCIATION with the forests and fjords
of Sweden, Julia and Oscar wanted no part of Adirondack wildlife.
Chipmunks would regularly invade Julia's kitchen, and her terror
and outrage were as voluble as if she had found a South American
bushmaster in the bread box.

"Oh, the Lord save me, Mr. Dunlap, there's a chipmunk in my

kitchen!" she would exclaim, bursting into the living room. "I saw it as I was washing the dishes. It ran right across the counter, not three feet from me."

Grandfather was prompt in assuring her that Oscar would make quick work of the beast with a rat trap. Indeed, Oscar boasted of his boyhood skill at running a trapline in Sweden, which he claimed earned him a small fortune in mink and ermine pelts. Yet his green and timorous revulsion in disposing of a dead chipmunk in the garbage would have led anyone to wonder whether he had ever set anything more lethal than the clips on Julia's earrings. On one occasion, however, his trapping skill did bring out a degree of manliness and ingenuity in him. He reported to Grandfather that raccoons were ransacking the garbage pit and strewing the woods with tin cans and dinner-table refuse. The pit, located beyond the powerhouse, was a large, well-constructed hole lined with boards and fitted with a metal trapdoor. A formal inspection by Grandfather confirmed that the coons had dug a hole beside the door and were making a nightly feast of ripe-smelling garbage.

"By heaven, Oscar," Grandfather pronounced, poking his cane into the hole, "we'll trap the rascal and make a camp pet of him. Damned if I don't think it a capital idea to have a tame coon on a leash about the place. And you'll take care of him, won't you, Bud?"

Now, it is true that when captured young, raccoons can make fine pets. But an adult raccoon is not such an amenable creature and with its fearlessness can be as savage as any beast. Not knowing this, Oscar and I set out a foot trap by the garbage pit. We felt sure the raccoon, once captured, could be transformed into a delightful pet merely by showing it affection and cultivating its taste buds with scraps from Julia's kitchen. Our anticipation was quickly satisfied. The very morning after we set the trap we were greeted by a fine, full-grown raccoon snarling and snapping at us in a most unaffectionate way. Oscar was not cheered by the sight: "Jesus, Bud, that's a mean fucking son of a bitch, that one." He picked up a stick and prodded the animal, prompting it to a further display of fury.

At this point the sensible thing would have been to fashion a cage and figure out how to get the creature inside, but neither Oscar nor I was sensible. Oscar decided he would lasso the beast while it was still in the trap. I was to pull taut on the rope as Oscar released it; after that, we would only have to drag the raccoon down to the icehouse and shut the door on it. The lassoing was supposedly the easy part of the scheme. Twirling the rope around his head, Oscar advanced on the hapless raccoon, crouched now in baleful but immobile ferocity by the garbage pit. Again and again Oscar cast his lasso, and again and again he missed the mark. Finally, in a burst more of impatience than of bravery, he crept close enough so that he all but dropped the rope over the animal's head, snaring one of its front paws as well.

Oscar was triumphant. "Now, goddamn it, Bud, you pull on this fucking rope until you damn near strangle the bastard, and I'll get ready to free it from the trap."

This was his moment of ultimate manliness. Shielded by a garbage-can lid he had retrieved from the powerhouse, Oscar slowly crept toward the trapped animal. "Now, Bud, for Christ's sake," he hissed at me as he neared the raccoon, "keep that son of a bitch rope taut and don't let the little bastard have an inch of slack, or by Jesus I'll kick your ass from here to Saranac."

Who was the more terrified—I, Oscar, or the raccoon—would have been impossible to determine. All I know is that I was pulling hard on the rope when Oscar shouted, "Hang on, now, Bud! I'm about to set the bastard free." The next moment, to my alarm, the rope went slack as the raccoon, free of the trap, made directly for me. Terrified, I dropped the rope and fled, escaping the onslaught of the raccoon only because it was still hobbled by the rope. Caught up in the drama of the moment, Oscar was on his feet shouting, "Oh, Jesus Christ, Bud! Don't let the son of a bitch get away!"

Oblivious to fear, he took after the raccoon, which by then was loping off past the powerhouse into the woods. Still brandishing the garbage-can lid, Oscar grabbed the trailing rope and gave a mighty tug. The raccoon whirled in its tracks and in fury charged him. There was a shriek of fright, the garbage-can shield went flying, and with an alacrity that would bring credit to a track star, Oscar took to his heels. Chastened by fear and humbled by our failure, Oscar and I stood side by side and watched that raccoon trot off into the forest. The rope was still about its neck, tangling in its feet. As it disappeared, its rump our last sight, it seemed small and ineffectual. But Oscar would have none of that.

"I don't care what your granddaddy says, Bud," he told me. "You can't tame a son of a bitch like that. Christ, I'd of whomped it one if I'd thought it was worth keeping. But, Jesus, who wants a critter like that? It's good riddance as far as I'm concerned."

NOT LONG AFTER THE AFFAIR of the raccoon, I turned my hunting skills to an entirely different species. Walking through the woods one day, I saw high up in a hemlock what appeared to be a large burl letting go with a stream of water. The burl, of course, turned out to be a porcupine placidly peeing. As many a summer camper has learned from pulling quills with pliers from the snout of a favorite dog, porcupines are everywhere in the Adirondacks. Their gustatory enthusiasms range from the siding on a wilderness shed to the varnished ribs and oars of a guideboat. Moreover, with the disappearance of the lynx and the decline in the fisher population, the porcupine's natural predators are almost nonexistent—except for murderous striplings like me.

For once Grandfather was disapproving of my bloodthirstiness. "Bud, you shouldn't kill porcupines," he said. "They don't do anyone any harm." But then, as so often occurred, he was taken with an inspiration. "By heaven, I'll tell you what! I've heard that men lost in the wilderness often survive by killing and eating a porcupine. That's just the ticket: we'll get Julia to cook one and see what it tastes like."

Now, at great sacrifice to her professional integrity, Julia had grudgingly compromised on the squirrel potpie. But when I appeared in her kitchen dragging by my belt a dead porcupine that smelled as ripe as the monkey house at the zoo, she exploded in wrath.

"Oh, God in heaven, what's that filthy thing you've got in my kitchen? *Augh,* the stink of it!" And then she saw the trail of blood on the floor. "Look here, young man, you get that thing out of here this minute. And I mean *this minute!* Then you come back here and clean up that mess on the floor. Get it out, now, get it out, or I'll have you by the scruff of the neck. Quick! Out the door, out the door!"

Only pride in my slaughter gave me the courage to stand up to Julia. "Grampa told me to bring it in here for you to cook."

"To COOK, did he!" As a sudden squall catches a sail and snaps it out in a ballooning surge of power, Julia visibly expanded as she was swept by a gust of outrage. Her head went erect, her bosom rose, and in a slow but deliberate movement she placed her hands on her hips.

"So your grampa told you I was to cook that thing, did he? Well, let me tell you, young man, you get that smelly porcupine out of here immediately and clean up that blood on the floor. And while you do that, I'll settle the business of cooking the filthy beast once and for all." With that she sailed out of the kitchen, through the pantry, into the living room, but her voice was still as clear as though she were five feet away.

"Mr. Dunlap, I've told Bud he's to get that porcupine out of my kitchen this minute or I take the next train to New York."

Sneaking into the pantry the better to eavesdrop, I suspected that for once Grandfather knew he had gone too far.

"Now, don't be angry, Julia. It's just a joke. You know, a little fun between Bud and me to see how you'd react."

"Joke, Mr. Dunlap! There's blood all over my kitchen floor, and it will take a week to get rid of that stink."

"Yes, yes, Julia, I know. But Bud will clean it all up, so don't fret yourself."

I was peering through the window of the pantry door and saw Julia aggressively tilt her head toward Grandfather, who as usual was seated at his desk.

"And about that cooking, Mr. Dunlap. I understand from Bud you gave instructions for me to cook the porcupine. Is that correct?"

"Well, you know, we thought we'd try it. Just as an experiment to see how it tasted."

"And you really thought I might cook it?"

Sensing the growing gravity of the situation, Grandfather tried a bit of sweet reason. "Well, you know, Julia, everything here in the forest is fit for human consumption. When you think of it, the animals probably have a cleaner diet than you and I."

"And that smell, I suppose, is just something that goes with their clean diet?"

"Well, I admit a porcupine does smell a little stronger than most. But think, Julia, many a man lost in the forest owes his life to eating porcupine. That's the honest truth. Ask George and he'll tell you."

But Julia, intransigent in her rage, was unimpressed. "Mr. Dunlap, if porcupine is such good eating to men lost in the forest, that's where they belong. Not in my kitchen."

Though daunted, Grandfather had still another stratagem. "Julia, I'm disappointed in you. For all these years I've said you were the best sport in the world. And now you're letting me down."

It was an ungentlemanly cut, and I suspect Grandfather knew it the moment the words were out of his mouth. There was a moment's silence, and from the rear I saw Julia's hands tighten at her waist. Then her voice, coolly measured, articulated each word with slow emphasis: "Mr. Dunlap, I've worked for you for nearly forty years, but when you ask me to cook a filthy porcupine, I can only say you're not a decent gentleman."

And with that Julia wheeled about and pushed through the swinging door, nearly catching me a nasty bump on the nose. Straight through the pantry and kitchen she marched, then out the screen door and down the wooden walk to the guidehouse.

Clearly this was a moment of crisis. When I joined him, Grandfather was torn between repentance and offense at having had his gentlemanliness called into question.

"Damn my soul," he intoned in his best Victorian biblical manner. "Looks like we've made a mess of it, Bud. Poor Julia, I never should have played on her so. But by heaven, there's a line to be drawn."

He paused a moment and then turned on me. "Bud, what did you do with that blasted animal? Get it out of the house, do you hear! I can smell the infernal beast all the way in here."

Within minutes I had dragged the porcupine out of the kitchen and deep enough into the woods to spare anyone the smell of its carcass. I returned just in time to see Grandfather, stone-faced, suit jacket buttoned, Panama hat on his head, proceeding down the walk to the guidehouse. Waiting for him to reappear, I was sick with disgust at my own uselessness and stupidity. I never wanted to hunt again. If I did, like a true wilderness scout I would kill, skin, clean, and cook my quarry alone in the forest. I was ashamed of the foolish storm that miserable porcupine had brought about.

Soon I heard Julia return from the guidehouse, the screen door slamming as she entered the kitchen. Just then Grandfather mounted the steps to the verandah, pulling his nose reflectively. Pausing for a moment he smiled and chuckled quietly. Noticing my long face as he entered the living room, he said, "Dammit boy, cheer up. Everything's all right; the world isn't going to end." His voice dropped, and he nodded in the direction of the kitchen, where Julia could be heard moving about. "Don't worry, she's fine. Between us we've made a pact: she'll only have to cook porcupine if I promise to eat it." He straightened to his full height and flicked his moustache in the manner of a duke about to give orders to one of his servants. "Don't ever forget it, Bud. A gentleman never makes a promise unless he intends to keep it."

SOME TIME AFTER the embarrassing raccoon and porcupine fiascoes, Grandfather decided the time had come for me to add my personal trophy to the Woodwil collection. At thirteen I had attained at least a titular form of manhood, if not legal adulthood. In Grandfather's eyes I was the last creditable scion of the Dunlap line, so it was mandatory that I take my place in the ranks of gentleman sportsmen. Thus, he decreed I must shoot a deer. The head, hide, and even hooves would be put on display at Woodwil. (Mounted on a board and bent at the ankle, hooves make excellent coat hangers or, better still, gun racks.)

If the end was a high calling, the means were deplorably low and sneaky. First of all, the only time I could possibly kill a deer was in summer, when I made my annual visit to Woodwil, and summer deer hunting was so out of season as to cheat on every bylaw of the sportsman's code. Second, no distinction would be drawn between doe and buck. As soon as I proved proficient with a high-powered rifle—I preferred the handsome .303 over the antique but venerable .30–.30— Oscar was to put out a salt lick. There, the deer would congregate in such numbers that, hidden away in a blind, all I would have to do would be to blaze away at random. How Grandfather was to circumvent the state game laws, let alone find a reputable taxidermist to mount my trophy, was one of those mysteries best left unexplored.

The .303 I selected for this deer-slaying venture was a lovely weapon, at least in my gun-crazed eyes. Weighing, I would guess, twelve or thirteen pounds, it had a fine walnut stock and a barrel of such beautiful tempered steel as to be positively erotic. Actually firing the .303 rifle, however, was a different matter entirely.

When the day came and Grandfather took down the .303, announcing that under his and Oscar's tutelage I would have my first target practice, I remember clearly the sudden fright weakening my knees. Still, when Grandfather gave the order to march, we marched. The line of march this time took us down one of George Donaldson's birch-lined trails a safe distance from Woodwil. The targets Oscar brought along were tin cans that he set up on a stump about thirty yards from the spot Grandfather had selected for my initiation into the rites of deer slaying.

Grandfather had designated Oscar to lead off the target practice, to show me by example how I should handle the .303. I had to hold the butt of the stock snug against my shoulder to reduce the kick of the recoil. I also had to place my cheek against the gun in such a way that I could accurately sight the rifle yet avoid the painful jolt as it kicked back. Astonishingly, Oscar proved himself not merely adept but close to a trained marksman. He loaded three lethal cartridges into the magazine, snapped the lever up and down to move the first round into the breech, and waited for word from Grandfather to commence firing. At Grandfather's command, *bang, bang, bang,* he fired three shots in rapid succession, and *plunk, plunk, plunk,* three cans went flying off into the woods.

Had I been less stunned by the shattering blast of the three shots, I would have been overawed by Oscar's unsuspected proficiency. But the explosive roar undid me. I was used to the comparatively civilized crack of the .22, not this earsplitting, mind-numbing blast. Moreover, I had seen Oscar's shoulder snap with the recoil of each shot. Amid the smoke and sharp smell of gunpowder, I am sure I visibly wilted. Sensing my alarm, Grandfather put his hand on my shoulder as Oscar was about to pass me the still-hot rifle.

"Now, take your time, Bud," he said kindly. "We've got all morning. This is your first time shooting a rifle as powerful as the .303. Oscar will help you out."

At best, I was a reedy sprite, and never did twelve or thirteen pounds feel so heavy as when I finally accepted the rifle from Oscar. Grandfather decided that because this was my initial exposure to such a fearsome weapon, I should fire only single shots and not use the magazine. Before I had any thought of firing, Oscar was at my side, showing me how to hold the stock tight to my shoulder and my cheek to the barrel for aiming. If the weight of the rifle had not been enough, my fright and nervousness sent the barrel waving around like a conductor's baton. As usual, Grandfather had the solution: Oscar would steady the rifle with one hand while I pulled the trigger.

Remarkably, the first two shots went off smoothly—if one considers that I did not faint and that no one expected the bullets to come anywhere close to the cans. It was the third shot that put a new slant on the whole deer-hunting enterprise. Because I had handled the recoil fairly well, Oscar suggested that I should fire unassisted, kneeling and resting the barrel on a convenient fallen tree. Indeed, it was just this posture that Oscar thought I should assume in firing at the deer herd congregating around the salt lick.

I knelt, rested the barrel on the tree, took what I thought was careful aim, and fired. The blast was shattering, in more ways than one. In my nervousness at firing unassisted, I had forgotten to hold the stock tight to my shoulder or place my cheek properly on the barrel. The recoil was brutal, all but dislocating my shoulder and giving my cheek such a nasty blow that, like Oscar with his smashed cheekbones, I too would surely have bits and pieces sliding around as loose as dice in a gambler's cup. With eyes blinded by tears of pain and fear, I looked to Grandfather for pity.

For all his stiff-upper-lip, spartan ways, Grandfather did have a gentle side. "You know, Bud," he said thoughtfully, "I think we better put off the deer hunting for another year, when you're a bit bigger and stronger. Don't you think so too, Oscar?"

As events turned out, there was not to be another year, and no befitting trophy of mine, other than the tiny red squirrel, would ever adorn the precincts of Woodwil. As a not unexpected corollary to that sorry target practice, I never again took quite the same relish in hunting. Oscar, however, with uncharacteristic tenderheartedness, took some of the sting out of my failure: "When you come to think of it, Bud, you got to be a real fucking son of bitch to want to kill a deer. Christ, even the meat tastes like shit."

 CHAPTER EIGHT

DESPITE ITS GREEN and gentle appearance, the Adirondack region is harsh, inflicting cruelty on humans as well as on the natural world. All too frequently one meets Adirondackers disfigured by some savage scar or lamed and bent as the result of an accident—a tree falling in the wrong direction, a snowmobile tipped over, a kickback from a chain saw. In middle age George Donaldson had both his legs broken when the huge sliding door of a railway car he was helping to unload fell off on top of him. During one of my boyhood summers a locomotive at a grade crossing struck and killed a guide at a camp near Woodwil. And one winter the dock chief at the Saranac Inn went through the ice while driving an automobile on the lake.

The remarkable thing is that with all the clearing of forest, road building, construction, and repair, I don't remember any calamities occurring at Woodwil. The only minor accident happened the day Boyce took off the top joint of his index finger while adjusting a belt on the Delco power plant. Oscar could do little more than replace a spark plug, so whenever something went wrong with machinery at the camp, he called on a mechanic in Saranac Lake or on Boyce, if he was there.

Perhaps because of severe illness in his youth, Boyce, a large, slow-moving man, never said an unnecessary word, preferring silence if that would do as well. When the flywheel belt lopped off the

112

top of his finger, he merely sucked in his breath, doubled over, and gripped the mutilated finger with his uninjured hand. When the first shock of pain had passed, he removed the plug of chewing tobacco from his mouth and methodically shaped it around the bleeding stub. Oscar and I, perennial kibitzers at all spectacles of mechanical genius, were horrified, but Boyce merely smiled in his gentle way and said: "Haven't you read your American history, Bud? Pioneers, you know, regularly used chewing tobacco as bandages. Kills all the germs and then some."

The nearest we came to disaster at Woodwil was my doing. During the clearing of Grandfather's woodland park Oscar took George and his crew back to the Saranac Inn each evening in the Chris-Craft. One night, when the launch was down with one of its periodic fits, Oscar took the five men across in the tin boat, their combined weight so heavy that the water lapped just inches from the gunwale. I happened to be out in the middle of the bay at the time, skylarking in the outboard. Now, to a thirteen-year-old boy in full possession of his witless villainy, one glimpse of the tin boat, barely afloat with its cargo of nonswimming mastodons, was enough to spark mischief. Gunning the engine to full throttle, I turned and, flying over the water, took dead aim at the midships of the tin boat. The men's reaction was all I had hoped for: shouting and waving in frightened pandemonium that I was about to hit them and doom each one to a watery grave, they for once were my pawns, and I was king of the lake.

I knew the outboard would turn on a dime, and not thirty feet from the tin boat I thrust over the tiller to avoid the collision. But what I forgot in the glee of my daredevil turn was that the wake from the outboard would be considerable. It burst over the gunwale and fell like a tidal wave on the panicked men. By some miracle the boat did not swamp and sink, but the engine conked out with a splutter, and the whole boatload of men stood soaking in the chill evening air.

Fortunately there was a pail in the boat to bail out the water. When, penitent and shamefaced, I drew alongside to offer any help I could, George paused in his bailing and, jaw muscles clenched in anger, looked at me levelly.

"I should tell your granddad about this," he said, "but I won't. But let me tell you one thing, Bud. Don't ever pull a damn fool trick like that again. There's not a man in this boat can swim, and you might have drowned us all."

Later, Oscar was consoling: "Jesus Christ, Bud, you should have known better. But, God Almighty, with the air tanks you couldn't sink that tin boat with an ocean liner. So forget about it."

George was more unrelenting, barely nodding to me for several days and limiting his greeting to a brusque "Hi, Bud." But I was soon welcomed back to the crew when, in a typically monosyllabic gesture of forgiveness, George asked me one morning to take a pail of drinking water to the men working in the forest.

THOUGH THE INCIDENT OCCURRED early in her childhood, it was my mother, the family member most disapproving of Grandfather's extravagance in building Woodwil, who was most direly affected by the harshness of the Adirondack climate. Woodwil, as I have said, was the second camp Grandfather built on Upper Saranac; the first was constructed in the 1890s on Gilpin Bay, some four miles down the lake. It was there that Mother, Boyce, and Jack spent their childhoods.

In order to supervise construction of the Gilpin Bay camp personally, Grandfather had housed his family in a tent that first summer. As so often happens in the Adirondacks, it rained the entire season. In the cold and wet, with primitive camp cooking and perpetually damp clothes and blankets, Mother contracted a feverish cold that lingered for weeks. Later that year that cold was diagnosed as rheumatic fever, a disease that permanently damaged her heart. Mother told me this story when she was forty-six, as the two of us walked one damp day in the Scottish Highlands. Three years later she would be dead.

Because of that early trauma, I don't believe Mother ever really liked the Adirondacks. True, she enjoyed the walks through the forest, the picnics, the clear, bright days when the mountains were sharp in the distance and the air was soft as lilac. But the frequent gloomy days, with the monotones of dark forest and misting rain, oppressed her.

She found her father, in old age, more difficult than ever. Like her two brothers, he had the maddening habit of calling her "Sister." Her real name was LaBelle, and she was beautiful—six feet tall, with auburn hair, and the same hooded eyes as Grandfather. Mother loved people, gardens, and arguments, so long as they were good-natured. She was forever on the move and was an uncompromising do-gooder, in the best sense of the word. Even back in the bluenosed thirties, she audaciously carried around birth control literature and condoms, ready to pass them out to anyone she thought unlikely to bring criminal charges against her. She helped found the first district nursing service to serve the poor in Nassau County, Long Island, and sat on the board of Bellevue Hospital. It seems to me she was forever taking under her wing alcoholic suburban males, failed actors and artists, refugee German furniture makers, and bankrupt stockbrokers.

None of these qualities were suited to Adirondack life, yet summer after summer she returned to look after me and a beleaguered old man, knowing the climate had irreparably shortened her life.

MOTHER'S MOST NAGGING FEAR for me was that I might drown. Like almost all Dunlaps, she was a poor athlete who positively detested sports of any kind. Of all the forms of exercise, she most disliked swimming. I remember that when Grandfather bought the sailing rig for the canoe, she wrote a panicked letter of protest. Grandfather threw it in the wastebasket with a contemptuous snort, citing it as further evidence of female irrationality. On her periodic visits to Woodwil she would quiz me as to what I would do if I were caught out on the lake in a thunderstorm or if the canoe capsized. She always ended the conversation with the admonition that I never leave the boat so long as it remained afloat.

Mother did have legitimate cause for worry. On blowy days, Upper Saranac kicks up a nasty chop that can easily overturn a light boat. With so many camps closed during those depression days and the number of tourists sadly depleted, the people likely to be out in boats who might see and rescue me were scarce. So when I and two companions (the only ones whom I liked out of all those Mother sent up to Woodwil) surreptitiously disappeared one night in the guideboat on a forbidden overnight camping trip, she was justifiably alarmed.

Grandfather's vision of a "rough camp" on Black Pond had so stirred my imagination that camping out became my obsession. Yet because of my asthma I was forbidden to spend even a single night in my pine-bough bed out at the end of the point. Mother feared that I might be taken with a seizure that could threaten my fragile life, but with the arrival of Harry and Bo, my two partners in crime, I gained the nerve to act on my fantasy.

I had long fixed on the site for our camping trip: Goose Island, a rocky islet about a half mile north of Grandfather's peninsula. It had a small cove to beach our boat in, a dozen or so windswept pines for shelter, and an ideal camping spot overlooking the cove. As ringleader I had planned our expedition with the sly will not only to outwit Mother and Grandfather but also to equip us with gear. My two friends and I shoplifted all our needs from Stark's hardware and the provisions store at the Saranac Inn. We deftly managed to come away with a splendid red kerosene hurricane lantern, a large five-battery flashlight, a small hatchet, a fine leather-handled sheath knife, and enough canned goods, candy, and other foodstuffs to see us out for a full week's expedition.

If the shoplifting required some ingenuity, choosing the day for our departure was simple, a matter of waiting until the adults had left for an afternoon's shopping in Saranac Lake. Within an hour we had taken down the tent on the point and loaded it, along with blankets, pots and pans, food for dinner and breakfast, and our trove of stolen goods into the guideboat, ready to shove off. But here competition bred anarchy. Who was to give directions? Who was to row? Who was to sit in the bow and keep watch? Though we were all of an age, Harry was pudgy and a good four inches taller than puny Bo, while I was little more than a reedy wisp. Still, it was Bo, the runt but the quickest wit, who made the assignments: Harry was to row, I to give directions (because I was the only one who knew where Goose Island was), and Bo to sit in the bow.

We left only a short note saying we had gone camping. (There was discussion of signing it in blood, but that idea was dismissed the minute we got a needle.) Once arrived at the island, we again fell into dispute, this time about who would do what. With an ounce of compromise we should have had the tent up, the fire set, and dinner cooked in plenty of time for the three of us to sit on the rocks, puffing on our cigarettes. For what was the joy of camping if we couldn't have three or four cigarettes each as proof of our ruggedness?

Come eight o'clock we were still arguing and shouting at one another that this was not the way to build a fire, that the hot dogs were gritty with ashes, and that the tent was positioned all wrong. Finally settling into our blankets for the night, we looked up to see clouds gathering in the west. At two in the morning those ominous clouds coalesced into a frigid thunderstorm that sent hailstones pelting against our fragile tent and water cascading from the rocks above to the ground under the flaps. But misery and discomfort are among the primary joys of camping, especially for the young, and after another bout of bickering we settled into a chilly, wet sleep.

That thunderstorm ignited Mother's terror and aroused all of Woodwil. When the adults had returned from Saranac Lake late in the afternoon to find our note, Grandfather had persuaded Mother, albeit reluctantly, that there was nothing to worry about in our adventure. Furthermore, it was too late to go searching for us, and when you came right down to it, our taking off on our own showed some real pluck. As for the asthma, I might be afflicted by it at home in the suburbs, but up here in God's country I had never been bothered by so much as a single wheeze. All the same, with the midnight thunderstorm my mother envisioned us three children being washed out of our campsite, packing up in confusion, and then, clad in only pajamas, taking to the water, where high winds and rough waves would surely overturn our boat.

At the first crash of thunder Mother rose, dressed, and, with a blanket wrapped about her, descended to the living room, where until dawn she waited in anguish. At five she woke Oscar, and at five-thirty they set out in the Chris-Craft in a cold and drizzling rain looking for the overturned guideboat. For more than two hours, moving slowly so as not to miss a single sign, they inspected nearly every known campsite on the lake—except the one we had chosen. It was at about eight-thirty or nine, after a disgusting meal of greasy eggs, bacon, and charred toast, when we packed up and set our oars for Woodwil. By then it had stopped raining, and though cold, wet and tired, we were jubilant with our adventure.

There was little celebration when we pulled up to the canoe ramp. Oscar was there to greet us. "Holy Jesus Christ, God Almighty!" he exclaimed the moment our bow touched the ramp. "Are you three ever in trouble! Where the hell have you been? And oh, my ass, are you going to get a licking from your granddaddy! And your mother, she'll string up each one of you to the nearest tree! Son of a bitch, you're really going to get it this time!"

The three of us, innocent little lads each, feigned shock at his eruption.

"Goddamn, Bud, if you're too dumb to know what you've done wrong, don't ask me to explain. All I can say is the three of you better get your asses quick as you can up to the main lodge. You'll find out soon enough from your grandpop what it's all about. All I can say is, you're in for a real pisser, and when I say pisser, I mean a real fucking pisseroo."

Mother, glued to the picture window of the living room ever since she had returned from her search of the lake, had seen us as we rowed into the boathouse and was waiting on the verandah. Even three brutishly insensitive boys could tell she had been weeping. "I think you had better go straight inside," she said unsmilingly. "Your grandfather is waiting for you."

Time has blessedly obliterated many of the details of our arraignment before Grandfather that morning. I distinctly remember, however, that as we entered the living room, he was standing by the huge fieldstone fireplace with his back to us, to emphasize to even our dim sensibilities that our crimes were so heinous as not to be countenanced in the sight of decent men. As we took our places in the middle of the carpet, he turned and, walking without his cane, launched into a litany of our thoughtless crimes.

Event by event he went over the ordeal of Mother's terror and suffering, his own deep concern, Julia and Oscar's troubled spirits. "Just think," he said. "What on earth could your Mother and I have said to the unhappy parents of these two boys if you all three had actually drowned? It would have been simply appalling!"

When we had not returned by eight-thirty that morning, he informed us, he had notified the state forestry service, and by now every fire watcher perched on lonely peaks from Lake Placid to Tup-

per Lake was looking for us. Not only that, he had been about to alert
Mr. Roosevelt's Civilian Conservation Corps, which might at this
moment have been mustering into platoons to comb the forest,
while the state police readied boats and grappling hooks to drag the
lake bottom for our bodies. When I look back on the incident, I question whether this alarm was ever sounded, but for the moment we
were properly chagrined.

There remained only the pronouncement of sentence to complete our arraignment. Then disaster struck. For at that moment, just
when the worst of our crimes appeared to have been recited, Oscar
burst through the swinging door from the kitchen bearing our stolen
booty. Grandfather's attention quickly focused on the large red
kerosene lantern. Now, as I have said, Grandfather was in certain re-
spects a parsimonious man. He was keenly aware of how each dollar
had been spent for the camp's upkeep, and it took only an instant for
him to decide that he had not authorized the purchase of such a
lantern.

"Where did that red lantern come from?" he asked, turning to
me.

I was not one to tell a lie. "Well, ah, it came from Saranac Lake."

"And from where exactly in Saranac Lake?"

Again the unvarnished truth, "Well, ah . . ." And then, knowing
all was lost, I blurted out, "I got it at Stark's."

"And how did you pay for it?"

"I didn't," I answered in little more than a whisper.

"Then how did you get it?"

"I just took it."

"You mean you stole it."

"Yes."

Surprisingly, Grandfather did not erupt in outrage or damnation.
But once the provenance of the lantern had been revealed, he quizzed
me on the five-battery flashlight, the sheath knife, and the hatchet.

Bo and Harry in turn were cross-examined, and they too were exposed as common thieves. There is no telling what our fate might have been had Grandfather been left to deal with us, but at that moment Mother intervened: "Father, I think it would be better now if the children were sent to their rooms while you and I discuss what's to be done."

Over lunch, limp as winded puppies, we heard our fate, which I am sure was Mother's idea. To impress upon us the full dimensions of our errant ways, we would individually be led before the store owners from whom we had stolen and there confess our crimes. At that point Grandfather, looking from one to the other of us, sternly described two possible eventualities. Either the store owners would report us to the police and have us hauled into juvenile court, or we would be required to pay for the stolen goods.

Miracle of miracles, whether it was because of our angelic faces or the store owners' deference to Colonel Dunlap, the merchants took back their wares after only the mildest rebuke. Even Grandfather seemed mollified by the store owners' show of kindliness and gave us only a token penance, one day's work around camp. With his penchant for the dashing gesture, he soon allowed our escapade to overshadow the disgrace of our shoplifting—after all, boys will be boys. On the night before Bo and Harry were to leave, in a break from a torrid game of dominoes, he leaned back in his chair and admiringly inspected each one of us.

"Well, you boys gave us an awful scare, but you're mighty good at picking a campsite. You know, I don't think there's a spot on the lake that's freer of bugs than Goose Island. The slightest breeze just blows them away."

Mother, reading by the only other electric light in camp, immediately looked up, startled indignation sparkling in her eyes. "Father, you're impossible! Here we raise the alarm of half the countryside for fear these boys are dead from drowning. Not only that, they make a disgrace of themselves by stealing. And all you can say is, isn't it wonderful they didn't get bitten by mosquitoes!"

THROUGHOUT HIS LIFE Grandfather had been sorely tested by adversity and tragedy. He had buried two wives and had seen his never-mentioned firstborn, Mortimer, die at age three. In addition, the health of two of his surviving children, Mother and Boyce, had been seriously damaged by early illness, and the third, Jack, though healthy, was hardly the apple of his father's eye. And finally, after surviving business setbacks and financial panics, Grandfather had been all but wiped out by the crash of 1929.

Perhaps this is why he admired nothing so much as grit and determination. He held a special regard for men who were resourceful in adversity. Highest in Grandfather's esteem was Matt Otis, the guide at his Gilpin Bay camp and the star of many of his favorite anecdotes. During the summers I spent at Woodwil, I met Matt Otis only two or three times, and by then he was retired and as old as Grandfather. He was a big man, with heavy, sloping shoulders of powerful muscles that in old age had gone to sagging flesh. He came by once, I recall, to discuss the building of the wilderness road in to Woodwil, and I shouldn't be surprised if it were he who had recommended George Donaldson to Grandfather. I was just a boy at the time, and I can't say Matt paid much attention to me—which is probably why I don't remember much about how he looked or acted, though for some reason I do remember his large, bony hands, mottled and corded with age. But the feature that stuck in my child's mind were his fingers and nails, blackened and coarsened as untanned leather by hard work and harsh weather.

Some forty years' acquaintance had cemented their friendship, but besides the loyalties time fosters, it was assuredly Matt's wiliness and shrewd practicality that appealed to Grandfather. He often repeated the story of how he and Matt had outwitted the game warden who came snooping around the Gilpin Bay camp on a rumor—true, of course—that Boyce or Jack had shot a deer out of season. Grandfather spotted the warden first and, via Boyce, sent word for Matt to hustle the deer out of the icehouse where it was hanging. The warden was no fool, and it took all Grandfather's wits to delay him long enough for Matt to disappear around the corner of the icehouse with the carcass just as the warden arrived for an inspection.

With the icehouse empty of evidence the matter might have ended there, had not Grandfather in one of his effusive gestures of pride decided to show off his camp. He elected to start with the guidehouse, which was exactly where Matt had chosen to drag the deer. As might be expected, Matt nearly fainted in consternation at the sound of voices as Grandfather and the warden approached. By a stroke of luck he had bolted the front door, so while Boyce made a great to-do over unlocking it, Matt escaped out the back door with the deer. According to Grandfather, this Hairbreadth Harry chase might have gone on all afternoon, except that Matt had the intelligence to deposit the deer back in the icehouse, which had already been inspected.

Matt won the hearts of Mother, Boyce, and Jack when he presented them one childhood spring with a gangling fawn he had captured in the forest after its mother had been shot out of season. All summer the fawn lived as a pet at the camp, in particular following Mother about because she was the one who fed and cared for it. When fall came, the grown fawn, by then as tame as a pampered lapdog, was killed by a hunter who probably shot it as it came up to lick his hand.

The most memorable story about Matt concerned his remarkable rescue, in 1903 or 1904, of Howard Bucknell, Howard's bride of ten days or so, and his brand-new mother-in-law. Mr. Bucknell was heir to the fortune that had endowed Bucknell University, and even as a naïve child in the early thirties I found him unremittingly pompous. A self-anointed woodsman, Bucknell was always seen wearing high leather boots that fitted snugly about his calves and laced to just below his knees. He wore a belt wide enough to support a broadsword, and a woolen lumberjack's shirt and hat so authentically backwoods as to be sold only by Abercrombie & Fitch. If not boasting about the largest lake trout he'd ever caught on Upper Saranac, he induced rigor mortis by telling how he had once killed a deer at nearly half a mile with his prized Mannlicher rifle.

At about six-thirty of a mid-May morning, when the mist was just rising from the water, Matt Otis was rowing a guideboat through one of the Fish Creek ponds on his way to the camp at Gilpin Bay. Suddenly he heard frantic cries for help. Several strong strokes of the oars, and through the mist he saw Mr. Bucknell and his two dear ladies thrashing about in the arctic water a hundred yards or more from shore. Mr. Bucknell was spending his honeymoon at his Upper Saranac camp and had decided to take his bride and her mother on a dawn fishing trip. In the wilderness of the Fish Creek ponds he had with his usual proficiency hooked a large and gamy pike and had artfully played the fish until he had succeeded in drawing it, exhausted, alongside his guideboat. Just as he was about to set the gaff, the fish gave a last powerful flip of its tail, sending up a geyser of water and panicking the ladies, who, in their frightened reaction, upset the tippy craft and plunged all three into the water.

Of the three, only Mr. Bucknell could swim, and even he was so weighted down by his Abercrombie & Fitch boots that it is doubtful he could have swum more than thirty yards. The temperature of the water in mid-May was such as to snuff out the life of the strongest swimmer in five minutes or less. The ladies were in a panic when suddenly, by heaven-sent coincidence, stout Matt Otis appeared. In seconds he rowed over and pulled them one by one to safety.

By further coincidence Grandfather and his two sons were at camp, and within an hour of the rescue they had the ladies and Mr.

Bucknell cozily seated by the fireplace, wrapped in blankets and sipping hot whiskey to restore warmth to their shivering bodies. By nine or so the Bucknell party departed for their camp with Matt in the launch, after a touching scene at the boathouse in which, according to Grandfather, Mr. Bucknell gripped Matt's hand and, fairly choking with emotion, swore that by the Lord's grace he was alive only because of Matt. No man, let alone his bride and his mother-in-law, owed more than he, Howard Bucknell, did to Matt Otis. He went on to say that he would be back that very afternoon for a word with Matt.

The anticipation at Gilpin Bay was enough to take away appetites. A dramatic rescue, a man of great wealth snatched from the jaws of death, and the hero, though poor, straight and true-tempered in mind and body! At the appointed hour Mr. Bucknell arrived and asked Grandfather for a word with Matt. Matt was summoned, and the two men disappeared for a short stroll up a path into the woods. They were gone no more than five minutes. Then Mr. Bucknell took a hasty leave of Grandfather, descended to the boathouse, and with a quick wave departed for his camp.

The moment Mr. Bucknell had covered a decent distance, Grandfather, Boyce, and Jack crowded around Matt. What had Mr. Bucknell said to him? What had he given him? An envelope! Well, for heaven's sake, man, take it out and let's have a look at it! Matt pulled the envelope from his hip pocket and with his finger tore open the flap. Inside was a sheet of letter paper, and inside the folds of that, a ten-dollar bill.

Later, Grandfather and Matt joked that the cheap reward was Mr. Bucknell's revenge for Matt's alacrity in rescuing his mother-in-law. But Grandfather, no college man, preferred to think it was one more instance of Bucknell's foolishness. "What the hell can you expect," he said, "from a man whose family was stupid enough to give money away to a college!"

CHAPTER NINE

MY UNCLES, BOYCE AND JACK DUNLAP, were big, good-looking men, the epitome of the well-brought-up, gentlemanly WASP. They had gone to Staunton Military Academy in Virginia, a reputable private school and to Grandfather something of a shrine because Woodrow Wilson had been born in Staunton and had gone on to Yale. The boys too went to Yale, though Boyce had to drop out in his sophomore year because of ill health. At Yale, Jack had joined socially proper St. Anthony's fraternity, and on graduation, with the United States entering World War I, had enlisted in the American Expeditionary Force Flying Corps, as the air force was then called. He never got so far as to be shipped overseas and was mustered out under something of a cloud—no one in the family ever knew why. In the meantime Boyce had suffered a streptococcal infection that rendered him, at least according to Grandfather, a semi-invalid for most of his life.

The brothers' early years marked them as respectable WASPs in more ways than one. For all their time at Staunton and Yale, they were woefully ill educated, like so many of their ilk. True, they had been dipped in the bracing waters of a liberal education, but the world of literate discourse remained as incomprehensible to them as Zoroastrian mysticism. If they read at all, they read newspapers, magazines, and best-sellers. In his youthful stock-brokering days,

Jack could talk a good line of financial-page jargon, and Boyce did fairly well by the operating manuals of various engines and appliances, but to ask either one to appreciate major works of art, literature, or music, let alone demonstrate a grasp of elementary science or history, would have blighted our respect for Yale.

Moreover, Boyce and Jack were crippled in a graver, more utilitarian way: both were incapable of earning a respectable living. Throughout his life Jack jumped from one crackpot scheme to another. Boyce was just too torpid and slow moving to do much more than chew tobacco and tinker with machines. As a result, for a good part of their lives and in particular during the depression, when earning a living was a challenge to even the shrewdest brains, they lived in large part off family charity. I can remember my mother passing along clothes, linens, even furniture to Jack and his family; as for Boyce, he was so stunned when Grandfather's well went dry that he became paranoid with conspiracy theories of how family members had bilked him of his rightful inheritance.

This is not to say that both men were not in their different ways attractive and engaging people. Jack in particular was an inimitable raconteur, and with his boisterous, infectious laugh he could keep a company of dinner guests entranced the whole evening. He was tall—just over six feet four—and good looking, and had a confident, debonair manner about him that could persuade the gullible that here was a man who could succeed in anything he undertook. On the other hand, Boyce—he too was tall, but burlier than Jack—was such a quiet, gentle fellow, with his shy smile and deferential ways, that you could not help but think him the soul of decency and good nature. In a word, although Jack and Boyce both had that unmistakable air of manners and upper-crust breeding, scratch the surface and there was nothing there but patina.

Psychologists would surely maintain that the source of many of Boyce's and Jack's problems was Grandfather's domineering personality. There is no denying Grandfather's role in sapping Boyce's vitality by keeping him, cradle to all but grave, on the dole and in indulging Jack's dreams of glory. He was always hard on them. If Grandfather lighted on me to compensate for some of his disappointments in life, maybe it was not so much my winning ways as an old man's grasping at a straw of reassurance, given the dismal careers of his sons, that life did have its small gifts as well as deprivations.

IT WAS DURING the first summer I spent at Woodwil that Boyce arrived—as usual for his annual stay—in the Buick sedan that Grandfather so favored for his ceremonial appearances at the Saranac Inn's porte cochere. The Buick, so far as I know, was the only thing of value Boyce owned, and if I remember the car so clearly, it is perhaps because in its inanimate way it resembled Boyce himself. It was a tall, boxy, ungainly-looking automobile, painted black, with an absolutely perpendicular windshield, a hood as foursquare and unadorned as a wooden crate, and a small trunk tucked modestly between the mudguards like buttocks squeezed at parade attention.

Like Boyce with his girth, this car was obviously not made for speed. Its whole appearance emphasized durability and dull utility. To the best of my knowledge, the Buick marked the only notable or exciting achievement of Boyce's life. He drove it twice across the country, and along the way found the only job I ever knew him to hold. In California he signed on as a Hollywood extra and spent two days in the High Sierra charging, with three or four hundred other men, back and forth across a snowfield, dressed only in an icy breastplate, tin helmet, sandals, and skimpy skirt. Typically, Boyce never learned the name of the movie, but I imagine it had something to do with Hannibal crossing the Alps.

If I portray Boyce as slothful and slow-witted, I should add that in his youth, before his illness, he was a stellar athlete. In football he was a star running back, in baseball a quick-footed infielder and batter. There were even occasions in adulthood when he showed the speed and decisiveness that marked his younger years. One rainy day, for example, while driving Mother and Grandfather to Saranac Lake, the Buick went into a skid and spun 360 degrees, heading straight for a telephone pole. Boyce, steady as a rock, steered the car skillfully out of the spin and, touching the brakes with a pianist's deftness, brought it to a stop just a whisker from crashing into the pole. So undone was Grandfather that he insisted on returning to camp. In shock, he lay down and waited for Mother to bring him a shot of bourbon, his cure for all the ills of the flesh.

The most tantalizing mystery about Boyce was why Grandfather supported him in aimless indolence for the better part of twenty years. Granted, in youth Boyce had been gravely ill. Yet by the time I knew him, he appeared a robust, healthy man. In chores around camp he was handy with an ax, had no trouble digging out and carrying the day's ice for Julia when Oscar was indisposed, and generally could make himself useful in operating and maintaining the equipment essential to our comfort. But for income he relied on Grandfather. Why Grandfather provided it, we never knew.

Of the two brothers Boyce was the more experienced, all-round woodsman, not that either was much of an expert on Adirondack flora and fauna. As youths on Upper Saranac, like most affluent young people, they were more interested in hunting, fishing, hiking, and overnight camping trips than in acquiring a naturalist's knowledge of the different trees, ferns, and wildflowers or of the habitats of mink and otter, grouse and deer. All the same, Boyce was the one who could tramp for hours in the forest and find his way home by dead reckoning. He knew the best places in the lake for bass and pickerel, could spot where deer had bedded down and recognize an osprey high in the air. He was a solitary soul and occasionally would disappear for the better part of a day, returning with a hatful of wild blueberries or raspberries. I particularly remember his coming home one day with a live fox in a gunnysack on the backseat of the Buick (there was no telling what odd paraphernalia he kept in the trunk of that car). He had spotted the animal caught in a foot trap just off a back road and, somehow freeing it, uncharacteristically had brought it back for me to see before releasing it. I say "uncharacteristically" because on the whole Boyce paid little attention to me at camp. When he did, the outcome was not always to my advantage.

He once sent me off on a harebrained hunt for frogs. As boys, he said, he and Jack had regularly fed feasts of frog legs to the family by going out at night with a flashlight, a fishing rod, and a bit of red flannel as bait. The trick was simple: when the frogs along the shoreline were setting up a deafening chorus—*rackety-ax, co-ax, co-ax*—you could take a canoe and stealthily paddle until the beam of your flashlight picked out a frog. Then you deftly flicked the red flannel past its snout and—voilà! you had a frog on your hook. A single night of trying this proved to me that handling a canoe, a fishing rod, and a flashlight—plus a piece of red flannel!—all at once was a trick that required the skills of a master juggler. Let me not even mention the mosquitoes. Still, assuming Boyce's scheme was feasible, he never did explain exactly who in the family was Francophile enough to instruct the cook in preparing frog legs.

Boyce did teach me two infallible methods for catching large-mouth bass and whitefish. Around the boathouse and off the rocks at the end of the point I frequently saw sixteen—and eighteen-inch bass gracefully cruising around like tiny dark submarines. By luck, I once successfully shot a splendid big one with the .22 when I spotted it basking on the surface. But none of my fancy lures, spinners, or night crawlers attracted more than passing interest from more cautious fish. And so it might have continued, had not Boyce one day seen me futilely casting off the point. Back then, before the invention of the spinning reel, bait casting was a fine art. Watching me pick away at a tangled line probably prompted Boyce to ask if I had ever tried cray-fish as bait.

Now, as I was to learn later, suggesting crayfish for bass was on the order of offering worms to a fly fisherman. But to Boyce, the point of fishing was to catch fish, type of bait be damned. Not long after our conversation, he returned from Saranac Lake with a cardboard box of crayfish carefully packed in wet pickerelweed. His technique proved close to miraculous. All I had to do was set my hook in the tail of a crayfish, toss it out into the water where the little critter could crawl around on the bottom, and within fifteen minutes, BAM, a three—or four-pound bass was on my line. In sporting terms it really was little better than dealing from the bottom of the deck, but, eager for suc-cess, I happily crossed this line.

The trick of catching smelt was another mark of Boyce's affinity with the soft underbelly of Adirondack deviousness. Smelt, which Grandfather regarded as next to ambrosia in taste, are smallish crea-tures that inhabit the deepest parts of freshwater lakes and are con-sequently difficult to locate and catch. But Boyce, artful woodsman that he was, suggested that with Oscar's help I bait a fishing buoy. That is, after finding a deep spot and marking it with a buoy—in this instance a short block of wood attached to a couple of sash weights—we should daily bait the area with chopped-up perch until we had lured a sizable gathering of smelt. After a few days of chumming we would need only to lower our poles to catch a fish among the assem-bled multitudes.

Oscar, not by temperament a fisherman, was immediately capti-vated by this idea, and so on Boyce's advice we located our buoy off a point a short distance north of Woodwil. For several days Oscar and I religiously baited our buoy morning and night. Finally impatience overtook us, and on a gray afternoon in a soft, drizzling rain we set off in the outboard to try our luck. We were well rewarded. Within five minutes of tying up to the buoy I pulled in the first whitefish, in another few minutes a second, and soon after, a third. Meanwhile, Oscar had not had a bite.

But that was just the beginning. As the afternoon wore on, I continued to pull in one smelt after another while Oscar sat there in growing sullenness and frustration. It was uncanny. He spat on his hook, exchanged rods with me, switched places in the boat, tried every hallowed ruse of fishing—all to no avail. It was almost an hour before he got his first bite, and longer before he caught his first fish. In fact, in the two hours or so we spent at the buoy, Oscar caught only three or four smelt while I pulled in fifteen or sixteen. All the while it was raining, a slow, cold drizzle that made a slight hissing sound on the surface of the lake, seeped into our shoes and down the neckbands of our ponchos, thoroughly wetting Oscar's cigarettes and matches so he had not even the consolation of smoking.

We never fished that buoy again: Oscar was suddenly too busy for anything so stupid as fishing. "Jesus," he said, "who wants to catch those goddamned little minnows? Might as well eat grubs as those fucking little bastards." As for Boyce, if he had to remain motionless for an extended spell, he preferred being supine in bed to sitting uncomfortably in a boat. Also, although smelt might be delectable, it turned out that Grandfather was just as happy to eat bass, and he never asked how either type of fish had been caught.

A BACHELOR until late in his thirties, Boyce had never been much attracted to women. Yet all at once, in the sluggish stream of middle age, his celibacy was simultaneously besieged by Mary Baker Eddy and a lady named Esther, who was of peculiarly determined righteousness. Esther wore a bun on top of her head and had a tongue marvelously adept at flattery. Where she came from and how Boyce's courtship blossomed are mysteries hidden away in the family closet. All I know is that during the second summer I spent at Woodwil, two and three times a week the mail brought Boyce a packet of pamphlets bearing the imprint of the Christian Science Church.

For some strange reason, in an establishment with eight commodious double bedrooms, Boyce and I always shared a room. Each night for a half hour before turning out the light, he was absorbed in those pamphlets. Then, one day a package came that was obviously not another batch of Mrs. Eddy's tracts. Soon afterward, Boyce's bureau displayed, next to his Bible, a framed photograph of a lady with a bun on top of her head and on her face an unctuous desire to please.

Esther came up to camp for her first visit later that summer. Any question of her intentions regarding Boyce were quickly resolved, not so much by doting eyes fixed on him but by her flattery of Grandfather. On arrival Esther feigned all but fainting spells in her admiration for Woodwil's beauty, and within a day, under Grandfather's tutelage, she could name each mountain observable from the verandah. On the ceremonial evening trips down the lake in the Chris-Craft, Esther declared each camp, though pretty, only second best to Woodwil. Julia's cooking was beyond compare, and Esther swore that her first night's sleep in the piny perfume and blissful silence of the forest was next to heaven. Soon Grandfather was so enraptured that her betrothal to Boyce was approved and blessed well before their nuptials. Indeed, when Esther took the unheard-of step of saying grace before dinner—she did, of course, ask Grandfather's permission—the words were in a sense merely a substitute for their wedding vows.

To Boyce, a lifelong semi-invalid, Christian Science offered the bloom of health through faith alone, without the nuisance of a single pill or vaccine. So if he seemed to fling himself into matrimony with Esther after a courtship devoted more to righteousness than to libido, good health was for him a goal worth pursuing. As far as I know, no member of the family attended Esther and Boyce's wedding, which took place the fall after Esther's first visit to Woodwil in a ceremony as discreetly private as the conduct of their courtship. Even after her marriage Esther did not cease her flattery of Grandfather. The couple spent their honeymoon at Woodwil. Within a week she wrote to Grandfather, in a letter he read aloud to Mother and me, that she and Boyce delightedly spent each evening by the fireside alternately reading aloud the Jefferson biography. Once he was Esther's wedded husband, Boyce, forsaking all others, seemed as married as any monk to the Christian Science Church. The only word we had of him was that he had become a "lay reader," and certainly his devotion was well rewarded in strength and good health for the rest of the biblical four score and ten years that he eventually lived.

In retrospect, Esther's fervent wooing of Grandfather should have served notice that more was buzzing about under that bun of hers than daughterly admiration. Woodwil, after all, suggested a family of more than ordinary affluence, and Grandfather, vain man that he was, was not averse to playing the role of opulent landowner. And had his largesse not supported Boyce for half a lifetime? In short, Esther had good reason to believe that with her marriage to Boyce, her piety might at last receive its just deserts.

Such harsh assumptions about Esther's expectations seemed confirmed barely two years later, when Grandfather died leaving a pitifully small estate. These were the dark, grim days of the depression, when manorial establishments such as Woodwil could hardly be sold for scrap and firewood. In the Adirondacks the splendid era of luxurious households staffed by numerous servants died quietly. The wealthy turned over the decaying hulks of their woodland estates to serve as children's summer camps, inns, and convention centers. Counting up the pittance that was Boyce's inheritance, Esther was transformed overnight from Saint Teresa into Medusa. She and Boyce had been robbed, swindled, fleeced, and flummoxed. Where was the money, the trust fund or annuity, to support her and Boyce in a manner befitting a scion of Woodwil? My father, who was a lawyer, had been named executor of the estate. But no bank statement or probate court accounting—which showed, incidentally, that Mother had forsworn in Boyce's favor what little sum she had been left—succeeded in mollifying the injured pair.

Eventually, Esther and Boyce were forced to accept that there simply was no large sum of money and that Grandfather had died all but broke. By then, however, the damage had been done; the split in the family was irreparable. In the same spirit of righteousness that they brought to Christian Science, Esther and Boyce wrapped themselves in unforgiving martyrdom. The one time I saw Boyce in the remaining years of his life was at my sister's wedding in the 1950s. He looked much the same, only older and, if possible, even blander. We didn't speak. He attended the church service and appeared just long enough at the reception to be noticed, and then left. Esther was not with him.

When Boyce died, Esther in an unlikely gesture to his by then inimical origins made a special trip to Upper Saranac to sprinkle his ashes on its waters. If I know my physics, in the millions of atoms forming a cubic inch of Upper Saranac water, there will forever be at least one particle of a Dunlap present. Befittingly, it will be a particle of the Dunlap who knew the region's lakes and mountains best.

IF BOYCE WAS THE MEMBER of his generation who knew the Adirondacks best, it was unquestionably Jack who loved them best. But during the summers I spent at Woodwil in the early 1930s, he had to love the region largely from a distance: for most of their lives, he and Grandfather were barely on speaking terms. The initial source of their falling-out was, I believe, the picture magazine Jack persuaded his father to finance soon after World War I.

In his day, as I've mentioned, Grandfather had been a leading trade magazine publisher. He sold out to McGraw-Hill in 1926, in-

tending to divide his retirement years between Woodwil in the summer and St. Petersburg, Florida, in the winter. He prided himself on
being a shrewd businessman with a keen sense of where the profitable markets lay. Jack, in contrast, was an enthusiast. Anything
with a whiff of the new and exciting, and he was on it like a beagle.
Entranced by the latest gadgetry of photography a good fifteen years
before Henry Luce launched *Life,* Jack talked the old man into in-
vesting heavily in a picture magazine devoted to business. Unfortunately, he lost his shirt in the venture, and he and Jack were never
really close again.

Though Jack's visits to Woodwil with his wife, Lorraine, and
small son John—John Robertson IV, no less—were rare and seldom
lasted more than a long weekend, what they lacked in frequency and
duration they made up for in zest. On one visit, for example, Jack
brought up an aquaplane, and we spent the better part of a weekend
being dragged a foot underwater behind the Chris-Craft. Still, when
he left, he swore, by golly, that on his next visit he would put a chair
on the aquaplane and sit reading the *New York Times* while Oscar
towed him around the lake.

Jack's was a boyish, infectious enthusiasm that made his visits a
celebration. On the picnics he organized we had ham or sirloin
steaks, not Mother's hot dogs and hamburgers. On night fishing parties for bullhead we went in the Chris-Craft, not in the tin boat or
outboard, with at least a dozen bottles of beer aboard. To ensure a
good catch, Jack would hang a lantern over the bow as a jacklight to
attract fish, a ruse that actually worked.

Jack's favorite Adirondack story about himself concerned the
time, some years earlier, when he and Lorraine had gone out to dinner at a neighboring camp. At close to midnight, on the bravado of a
snootful of bourbon and the tall tales of his hunting exploits, Jack
announced that if his host would lend him a .30–.30, he would go out
and get a deer before dawn. The host, also far gone in whiskey and the

magic of Jack's stories, immediately complied. It was only in the throbbing, bleary-eyed, first glimmer of daylight, with not a sign of Jack about, that the host realized the folly of the night's drinking and so, rousing the household, organized a search party. Surely Jack, tanked up and thrashing about in the black midnight forest, had stumbled and shot himself, tripped and broken his leg, or fallen into a bog of quicksand. Led by the panicked host still clad in pajamas and bathrobe, the searchers had hardly gotten three hundred yards into the forest when they found Jack, slumped against a tree trunk, cradling the .30–.30 across his lap, as sound asleep as Little Boy Blue.

Despite the fun and games, Jack's visits to Woodwil were marked by the uneasy tension between him and Grandfather. In his ebullience Jack talked and laughed too loudly, wanted that extra splash of whiskey just as Julia was about to serve dinner, or over the evening's dominoes and cribbage would turn on extra lights that Grandfather was sure would drain the power-plant batteries. In the Chris-Craft, Jack would open up at full throttle when Grandfather urged caution. There was the cigarette butt that Jack casually flicked into the woods when Grandfather was not sure it was entirely snuffed out, the chair moved to the verandah from its accustomed place, the swimming towels not picked up, the wet feet padding about the living room. Taken singly, these peccadillos were trivial, but in concert, or even in twos and threes, they generated friction between father and son. Nothing ever exploded into open rancor, but after three days of a long weekend the turkey wattles at Grandfather's neck seemed to tremble in precarious control, and his eye had a look of angry but resigned suffering.

Given this at-best edgy truce, Jack did not come into his own at Woodwil until after Grandfather's death. By that time Boyce was far gone in Christian Science, so for the latter part of the 1930s and 1940s Jack could play lord of the manor, with no one but my father, as Grandfather's executor, to take so much as a supporting role.

There being no money to maintain the place, summer rental of the camp provided the only cash for its upkeep. Still, in spring and fall, Jack, largely unfettered by regular employment, could enjoy Woodwil as his own. He presided over the essential maintenance work, and what he could not afford local hands to perform, he did himself. Julia and Oscar were no longer there to cook and keep house, and when rentals shrank during World War II, a creeping shabbiness, aggravated by the merciless climate, overtook Woodwil. Despite peeling bark on the handsome log trusses, faded stains on the walkways between buildings, and the generally tacky look of furniture and furnishings, Jack still had the stunning view down through the Narrows and the panorama of mountain and forest to inspire a sense of lordly possession.

With age Jack grew to look more and more like his father—the same narrow forehead, the hooded eyes, the fleshy, slightly hooked nose. (He did, however, retain some hair on his head, and lacked the small bristly moustache Grandfather had favored.) Jack was proud of the likeness, and after shaving he would frequently look in the mirror and with a mock salute say, "Hi, Dad" or "Good morning, Pop."

Jack's greatest success came in finding and delivering to the camp a splendid secondhand 250-horsepower Chris-Craft to replace the *Arodasi,* which by then lay on the bottom of the lake. In taking charge of Woodwil, Jack persuaded my parents that a speedboat was an essential selling point in renting the place. He had located just the boat, unfortunately named the *Mitzi,* at a marina in Sheepshead Bay, on the Brooklyn waterfront. Thus began what I think of as Jack's Siegfried idyll—a sublime trip in the *Mitzi* up the Hudson, through the canal to Whitehall, New York, then to Lake Champlain and finally to Westport, where it was taken out of the water and hauled by truck over the mountains to Lake Placid and thence to Upper Saranac. In his waning years, with a sigh of nostalgia, Jack would recall speeding past the Gothic battlements of West Point, the holy shrine of Hyde Park (unlike Grandfather, Jack was loyal to Roosevelt to the end), the ostentatious Vanderbilt and Livingston mansions, and, moving up Lake Champlain, past Fort Ticonderoga to enter at last the glorious sweep of the Adirondacks. A bit awash in whiskey, he would slap his thigh and, fixing me with a slightly mad look in his eye, exclaim that we would all join him in doing it again. With our wives and children we would rent a houseboat on Champlain and for a month cruise its length, from the Canadian border in the north to Putnam Station near its southern extremity. But, alas, by that time Jack could hardly afford a bus ticket to Westport, let alone a houseboat with accommodations for eight to ten people.

As might be expected, Jack brought to the banal tedium of earning a living the same ebullience he did to his treasured Adirondacks. As might also be expected, he met with the same dismal results. In a business career that spanned the years from the mid-1920s to the 1950s, he promoted schemes to market a chocolate drink called the Brown Bomber—to be endorsed, naturally, by Joe Louis (I doubt that Louis was even approached)—and to sell advertising on New York City subways. In this latter venture the plan was that at each stop a recording would tout the merchandise of local stores. Soon after Prohibition was repealed, he persuaded my father to bankroll him in a venture to make applejack in a small distillery on the Hudson. Not even the orchard growers whose apples he bought could be persuaded to drink the stuff.

In the predepression 1920s, Jack did have a moment of glory as a stockbroker on Wall Street. With typical flamboyance he showed off his success with a fancy house in New Canaan, Connecticut, complete with swimming pool and Cadillac, along with a thirty-five-foot cabin cruiser. But he was never much of a broker. Before going abroad with my family one summer, my father left Jack to watch over a hot tip in which he had invested. How satisfying it was to my father to see that stock steadily rise, week after week, until it appeared that our whole trip would be paid for by the profits alone. At the pier to greet us on our return, however, was Jack with the news that not two weeks after our departure he had got jittery and sold the stock, with peanuts for a profit. Was there a hint of contrition, a word of mea culpa, "God, Kenneth, how sorry I am!"? No, just a comradely slap on the back and the devil-may-care reassurance, "Well, you win some, you lose some."

My father was a cautious lawyer, yet even he could not resist some of his brother-in-law's schemes. During the war Woodwil declined into woeful disrepair, to the point where major rehabilitation, including a new roof for the main lodge, was critical. As executor, my father was presented with a grave decision: Should he abandon the camp to the county for taxes or, risking his own financial well-being, borrow money for repairs on the forlorn hope that once refurbished, Woodwil might still attract renters and eventually be sold? In short, Woodwil had become a white elephant. At this point Jack, shocked by the decisions facing my father, stepped forward. "Kenneth," he told him, "there's a simple way out of this mess. There's a small fortune in timber on that land, and all we have to do is lumber it and you'll have cash galore to put the place in first-class order." In no time bids were let out to lumber the property, and for once Jack appeared to be right: the proceeds promised would more than pay for repairs to the camp—reroofing, new siding, painting, the lot. But there lay the trap: so plentiful and so easily got seemed this money that Jack proposed that he be the contractor. He would rent the necessary equipment and hire local labor on the cheap: "Kenneth, I swear to God, we can make a goldmine!"

My father fell for it. A small sawmill was rented and cheap labor hired. In a scam as old as the country bumpkins taking the city slicker to the cleaners, those stalwart, native Adirondackers lined their own pockets by selling off the best lumber on the sly and leaving Jack with scrap that would barely pay for the roofing nails.

Two or three years later my father succeeded in selling Woodwil, plus ten acres of the roughly fifty, for $25,000. It was a good price—if one ignores the fact that Grandfather had spent more than $200,000 back in 1926 to build it. But money aside, the saddest part of losing Woodwil was seeing the wanton destruction of Grandfather's woodland park. Even today, fifty years later, the scars of Jack's failed venture remain evident in the scrub brush and rotting stumps where giant hemlock, spruce, and pine once stood.

In form and substance Jack has always seemed to me the last Gatsby, that image of stylish twenties recklessness and boyish charm. And today when I walk through what was Grandfather's park, any outrage I feel is softened by the realization that this is the way it had to be, the way Scott Fitzgerald would have plotted the denouement of Jack's love of Adirondack lakes and mountains.

Jack's death was of a piece with the way he had lived. For years, according to Lorraine, he was morbidly convinced he would die of cancer. When he began to feel ill, he refused to see a doctor. Finally, he became so debilitated that he was forced to enter the hospital. Ironically, doctors diagnosed his illness as acute nephritis; had he been treated earlier, there was every reason to believe he could have made a complete recovery. Once more the victim of an unlucky bet, he died in a veterans' hospital, far from his beloved Adirondacks.

# CHAPTER TEN

IN OUR EVERYDAY LIVES there are two types of memory: that of the specific, narratable incident that we remember because of its impact on ourselves and others, and what I call the sudden, unprompted still life of an isolated moment. All at once, in a split-second vision we are back, in all five senses, at a spot we see in our mind exactly as it was twenty, thirty years ago.

My most vivid still life is the sight of the living room at Woodwil at seven-thirty of an early May morning. At that time of year it was often cool, and to take the chill off Oscar would build fires in the fieldstone fireplace and in a mammoth metal stove that stood at one end of the room. I slept in one of the two bedrooms that opened onto the long balcony overlooking the living room. For the first two or three weeks of each summer I woke to the strong, acrid smell of those two fires crackling and popping in the room below. When, still in pajamas, I stepped out onto the balcony under the spreading roof, there in front of me was a child's ideal world: the snap and hiss of the fires, the sharp smell of smoke, the cold morning air, and, beyond the picture window by Grandfather's desk, the misting lake and the dark humps of the mountains in the distance. Today, more than sixty years later, that scene is as vivid to me as it was to a twelve—or thirteen-year-old boy still rubbing the sleep from his eyes. Nothing stirs in this picture; no bald eagle flies low over the flagpole. There is no sign of Oscar climbing onto the rock ledge to put up the flag, no sound of Julia shaking down the coal fire in the kitchen stove. It is simply a vision frozen in memory, but so alive as to have its own eternity, so sudden that for an instant it re-creates the emotions of joy and delight that infused a boy's heart.

For several years in a row I was taken out of school two or three weeks early so I could accompany Grandfather to Upper Saranac to open Woodwil. Many a modern educator would be shocked at such disregard for education, but, mindful of that vision of the living room on a May morning, I am convinced that Mother and Mark Hopkins were essentially of one mind: there is no finer classroom, at least metaphorically, than a log in the forest with the pupil at one end and the teacher at the other. In this instance my Grandfather was the teacher, despite all his prejudices and a mind shaped in a different century.

Another picture that comes frequently to mind is that of joining Oscar at dawn to meet someone—Mother, a guest—arriving at the Saranac Inn station on the overnight sleeper from New York. The railroad station was a squat building set off by itself at the end of a small meadow, hemmed in on all sides by forest and so unprepossessing that a solitary passenger, unmet, might well have felt himself abandoned in the wilderness. We always arrived at least twenty minutes early so that Oscar, starved for conversation with someone other than Julia or me, could step inside for a few windy exchanges with the stationmaster. I stayed outside, either walking tightrope fashion on the rails or flinging stones from the gravel platform high into a grove of birches on the far side of the tracks. Occasionally, just before the train arrived, another car might pull up and a man or woman would get out. Struck silent by the solitude of the station and the fresh, golden light of early morning, they would pace up and down the platform.

Then came the magical moment when down the tunnel of forest

bordering the tracks would come the forlorn, hooting wail of the train whistle. The sound still reverberates in my mind as it slowly peaks and the fading notes drift off to die in the vast silence of the woods. Hard on the last notes of the whistle, the rising thunder of the train, far down the tracks, would set the forest alive with noise until in a sudden explosion the locomotive with its long, swaying line of cars would burst into view in a swirling cloud of steam and smoke. With sparks leaping from the great driving wheels as the brakes were applied, car after car would flash by, windows shrouded with curtains. On the platforms between cars, the porters would stand with metal steps in hand to place on the ground for descending passengers.

I don't suppose it took more than a minute from the time the train burst out of the forest until it came to a stop, but half an age, it seemed, of excitement and wonder passed through my mind in those few moments. The shattering noise of hissing steam and steel grinding on steel was beautifully exciting, and each car as it passed seemed a curtained mystery. But, most of all, the sudden transition from wilderness solitude to rude, blasting intrusion creates the immediacy of the scene in my mind today. The memory is animated by no particular guest's arrival; the whole vision, like the first mournful sound of the whistle, is isolated in its own timeless reality. (Although it's likely that, just as the train slowed to a stop, Oscar would materialize at my elbow and pull me away from the tracks, shouting: "Jesus Christ, Bub, get back, get back, or that goddamned thing will suck you under the wheels!")

Finally, I carry a picture of Grandfather in the evening over a game of dominoes. Almost every night, immediately after dinner, he would tell me to get out the card table, the box of dominoes, and the pegboard. These I would set up under the lone wicker floor lamp that, with both bulbs lit, shed just enough light for a keen-eyed player to decipher the dominoes in front of him. Grandfather's set, in keeping with the grandeur of Woodwil, was made of solid ivory and was housed in a mahogany box with a sliding top so expertly fitted that when it was shaken not a rattle emanated from the dominoes inside.

The scene is vivid to me. Once seated, with his gold Seth Thomas pocket watch carefully placed on the table at his elbow, Grandfather looks across at me as I shuffle the dominoes, his hooded eyes alight with a crafty insult. "Well, young man, how many points do you want me to give you tonight? I'll tell you what; I'll give you twenty-five points the first game, and for every ten points I beat you, I'll add five more on the next game." Each hole on the pegboard is worth five points, and with a good eighty to one hundred holes for the round trip up and back down the pegboard, twenty-five points isn't all that much of a handicap. All the same, the competitive put-down is made all the sharper when he next asks, "And how much money have you got in your pocket tonight for me to win?" He taps the Seth Thomas with his forefinger. "We've got until nine-thirty," he announces, "so you better be lucky, or I'll take you for every penny."

The competitive edge Grandfather gives our games greatly increases their excitement. Not only might money be won or lost, but against long odds a triumph might crown me David the Goliath slayer. Best of all are the times I succeed in sending Grandfather to the "boneyard"—that is, when he has no domino in his hand that he can put into play and is forced to draw from the tiles turned face-down on the table. For an instant when this occurs, Grandfather, unbelieving, surveys the dominoes lined up in front of him, absently sucking and pushing on his lower denture with his tongue until his lip, jutting Hapsburg fashion, nearly meets his nose. Realizing he is indeed blocked, he explodes in properly theatrical indignation: "Why, you young scallywag, send me to the boneyard, will you?!"

In a lofty, majestic movement he extends his hand over the face-down dominoes, holding it motionless while with slow deliberation he ponders his choice. The yellow light of the lamp makes the skin on the back of his hand, mottled with brown liver spots, look as pale and fragile as tissue paper, but the thumb, with its long, arrogant curve, is raised in defiance of my ploy. He makes his selection and picks a domino that will give him a chance to score or, in retaliation, send me to the boneyard. The hawk-beaked thumb leaps up in triumph an inch or two in front of his nose. "Now, you rascal," he intones with mock ferocity, "let this teach you, you can't send an old man like me to the boneyard without paying the price!" He plunks down the domino and sits back squarely in his chair, waiting for my despairing expression at the genius couched in the luck of his draw. In the lamplight he seems immensely old, the skin so tight and thin across his brow that I can see the faint blue tracery of veins below, his deep-set eyes watery with age.

AFTER FOUR SUMMERS at Woodwil, the world I knew there, the one reflected in these memories, ended abruptly. For the two years remaining to him, until his death in 1935, Grandfather rented out the camp and spent his summers migrating from the Saranac Inn to our house on Long Island and from there to the old Vanderbilt Hotel, on lower Park Avenue in New York City. Considering his dwindling resources, I suspect he was not a little thankful to be relieved of the burden of maintaining Woodwil in the style he felt essential to his own and the camp's dignity. To him, Woodwil was never merely a summer home; in it was bound up his image, whether real or illusory, of the landed Kentucky bluegrass heritage destroyed by the Civil War. In old age, twice widowed and alienated from his sons, Grandfather had made Woodwil his justification for living. He poured money into it that he did not really have in order to maintain a standard of living no longer relevant. By renting, he was surrendering to other hands the landowning tradition that was to a degree his ultimate moral code.

Yet for all this sacrifice, there was no apparent diminishment of the one trait in him that would have been death to hide—his incomparable patrician arrogance. I remember his arriving at our house one spring day puffed up with pride and boastfulness, displaying an edition of the newspaper from St. Petersburg, where he had spent the winter. In it was an interview with him, complete with picture. Why the paper should have wished to interview Grandfather I cannot imagine, except that in those depression days the winter resort lacked anyone else of much interest. The paper, however, got more than it bargained for: Grandfather expatiated on his favorite theme of blue blood and the natural genetic superiority of the Anglo-Saxon peoples. Bowdlerized as the final version of the interview undoubtedly was, Grandfather was as oblivious as a rhino to any offense he might have caused readers. After all, it was only the truth, the unvarnished truth, he was telling.

In those grim days of the mid-1930s it is testimony to his promotional talents that Grandfather was able to rent Woodwil at all, much less for the two full months of the summer season. One tenant, unaccountably, was a group of Jesuit priests. Whether the fathers were using Woodwil as a retreat for meditation and prayer or merely for recreation is unrecorded, but one effect of the rental was to raise Grandfather's opinion of that order in particular and, by association, of a small mite of the Catholic Church at large.

The only other notable outcome of renting out Woodwil was the episode in which Oscar threw the potbellied stove from the guidehouse into the lake. It all came about when a tenant presented Julia and him with a generous one-hundred-dollar tip at the end of his stay. Julia, naturally, wanted to sock away the full amount in their savings account; Oscar, in wanton celebration of summer's end, snitched ten dollars and departed for Saranac Lake for a couple of bottles of whiskey. On his return he proceeded to get stupefyingly drunk. From there one thing led to another, first hurling obscenities and curses at Julia, then smashing glasses and dishes, then swaggering about Mother's lawn brandishing one of Boyce's .38 revolvers—and, finally, jettisoning the stove in the lake. During it all he shouted denunciations of Grandfather, threatening at the top of his lungs that if that goddamned, stuck-up old bastard weren't such a feeble, useless son of a bitch, he'd punch him in the nose.

Fortunately, George Donaldson and his younger brother, Harold, were working in the woodland park and, hearing Oscar's hullabaloo, hastened over to see what was wrong. Down to the guidehouse they went to subdue Oscar in any manner they could, a task they accomplished without so much as laying a finger on him. In rough fellowship they invited themselves to a drink with him and then so spiked his glass that he passed out in sobbing self-pity after several swallows.

The incident with the stove was the only time I ever heard of Oscar getting drunk. True, he once in a great while smuggled a bottle into the powerhouse. On especially audacious occasions, and after much scratching of his crotch, winking, and prodding me in the ribs, he would dig it out of its hiding spot among the batteries for a quick snort. And once or twice when we returned from shopping in Saranac Lake, his landing of the Chris-Craft would be more inept than usual, and he would step out of the boat with breath like a blowtorch. But for that down-to-earth, hairy-chested drunkenness, I missed the 100-proof demonstration.

Perhaps it's just as well. I like to remember Oscar for his less profligate sins: his simple relish of profanity, the small lie, the paltry but purposeful miscalculation in counting change. His charm lay in his uncouthness; he really did enjoy farting, and there was a kind of sweet perfume to his rank, utilitarian aroma of sweat and gasoline. I loved him for his rascality and laziness, those qualities that, if we are honest, we find mirrored in ourselves. In him they were made almost admirable by his frank admission of them. Most of all I loved him for the attention and companionship he gave me at a time in adolescence when we are most insecure and alone.

After the episode of the stove I saw Julia and Oscar only once or twice again, during short visits to Woodwil. When Grandfather died, they disappeared from my life entirely. I am sure Mother saw Julia right up to her own death in 1939, but it never occurred to me, with the selfish neglect typical of youth, to look them up or even to find out what eventually happened to them. I am confident that so long as Julia's Nordic inner will stayed with her, no great harm came to them.

They too feature in those mysterious still lifes of memory that occasionally occur to me: Oscar in the boathouse tinkering with the engine of the tin boat or out on the lake in the early evening, rowing the guideboat while I troll. Julia, hot and perspiring in the kitchen, cursing the coal stove or, after dinner, the cooking and washing done, marching down the wooden walk to the guidehouse, her shoulders set square and defiant, placing one foot in front of the other with a stern confidence that, had her sex been different, would have made her a Viking warrior. In those summers at Woodwil I crossed the shadowline between childhood and early adolescence, and certainly good fortune and all my tutelary deities smiled kindly on me in sending those two persons to watch over me.

GRANDFATHER DIED at the end of July in 1935, at the French Hospital on West Thirtieth Street in Manhattan, having sold not a single lakefront lot on Upper Saranac. Early the previous winter he had been operated on for prostate cancer, and I remember going with Mother to see him in the hospital. Naturally, he had a private room, and strewn about the chairs, bureau, and window seat were at least a

week's editions of the *New York Times*. Thanks to the holes he'd created by clipping out articles, the papers looked like a madman's sten-
cil. Grandfather had always been a fanatical newspaper and
magazine clipper, and at Woodwil, when he wasn't writing letters to
clergymen in Inverness for baptismal or interment records, he could
be found on the verandah chopping up the *Times*. He then dispatched
these clippings to friends, congressmen, senators, governors, and
what-have-you, attached with a pin to short handwritten notes. (Unless you knew better, chances were your forefinger would be cruelly
lanced in opening one of his dispatches.) Mother and I were barely inside the door of his room before he was ordering his nurse in a sten-
torian voice to fetch him that batch of clippings he had asked her to
set aside for his son-in-law Kenneth Spence.

Then, having had no suitable audience since Mother's last visit,
he was off on a diatribe against Hitler, Mussolini, or whatever public
figure had lately fallen in his eyes to an estate lower than that of a lily
picker. Having disposed of the politicians, his next targets were his
doctors. To take care of his plumbing, he had been equipped during
the operation with an external tube and attached rubber bag that I
suspect deeply humiliated him. Being a boy, I was intrigued and
wanted to inspect this ingenious contraption, but in an era when
even the toilet was unmentionable in polite society—my father,
with great delicacy, regularly called it "the twilight"—Grandfather
was not about to let me see it. The indignity of the tube and bag
surely reminded him of the decay and detritus of his declining life.
Racked by pain and fear, he cursed his doctors, the bad food, and the
inefficiency of the nurses. In a half hour's visit he uttered hardly a
pleasant word, and when we came away, Mother made no secret of
her concern over his impending death.

Discharged from the hospital, Grandfather departed as usual for
St. Petersburg. When he returned in late April, it was evident from
his frailty that he had not long to live. Instead of going up to open

Woodwil for the new summer tenants, he sent Mother. Like an old wolf wanting to be alone in the indignity of death, he refused to stay with us in the suburbs for longer than a day or two, and left grumpily and in pain for his rooms at the Vanderbilt. There he remained until he entered the hospital for the last time, just after the Fourth of July.

Originally my father had planned that he, Mother, and I would spend July motoring to Dallas to visit his brother. But with Grandfather's illness the trip was canceled, and, to my shame, I was quite put out. I did go with Mother to see him one last time, a week or so before he died. He was strangely gentle and quiet, and lay in bed with the sheet pulled high up on his chest, the hem of which he kept folding and refolding with fidgeting, wasted hands. The weather was stifling, and because there was no air conditioning in those primitive days, he had removed his toupee, which made him look even more cruelly old.

I have no recollection of a funeral or service, though there must have been one. I do remember that Mother and Jack took his body on the train to Lexington, where he was buried, the last of his immediate family to return to rest in Kentucky. Years later, in the early 1950s, my wife and I and our children, on the way from Chicago through eastern Kentucky and the Smokies to North Carolina, stopped for the night in Lexington. I thought to go look for his grave, but it was too late in the evening, and we were committed to an early-morning start. In a sense Lexington seems the natural place for Grandfather, home from the hill, back to the rich, horse-breeding bluegrass region, side by side with numerous other Dunlaps. But to me his spirit will always walk the forest around Woodwil, limping down birch-lined paths long overgrown, among tall pine and hemlock felled years ago.

To compensate for the canceled Dallas trip, in late August my father took the family on a two-week fishing trip to a private club in the Laurentian Mountains, north of Québec City. For my father, urban from the top of his derby hat to his wing-tip shoes, this excursion was as out of character as a Caribbean vacation for an Eskimo. Clearly he had planned it as a balm to Mother and me for Grandfather's death. But the night of our arrival at the club, for the first time ever in the high, clear air of mountains and forest, I was seized by such an acute asthma attack that I had to be hospitalized. For the second time a trip was canceled, and my father and brother returned to New York, with Mother remaining at the hospital in Canada while I recuperated. Perhaps a bout of severe asthma occurring in an Adirondack-like region was a simple coincidence, but perhaps too, in spite of my apparent unconcern, it was caused by the subterranean workings of my psyche over the death of that magnificently irritable, domineering old man only a month earlier.

ALMOST IMMEDIATELY following Grandfather's death, my father put Woodwil on the market, but it was not sold until shortly after World War II. In the intervening years my father chafed under the responsibility of trying to maintain the camp in more or less saleable condition. Just before the United States entered the war, however, in a quixotic gesture to Mother's memory as well as to Grandfather, he invited a good part of the family for a long weekend at the camp. By then he had remarried and gained in the bargain two young stepsons.

It was a gala occasion. He brought up a cook and a housemaid on the train from New York, and in order to miss as little as possible, Jack and Lorraine drove all night from Greenwich, Connecticut, arriving at about five in the morning. Jack especially went daft with the joy of being back at Woodwil in the style and with the personal service he felt due a Dunlap on his family estate. Throwing off the weariness of the long drive with the first scent of heady Adirondack air, he tried to re-create a summer's activities in the three days he was there. We went aquaplaning, had a picnic down the lake on Buck

Island, and fished for bullhead at night, again with a lantern over the bow of the *Mitzi*. We shot at targets with the same .22 I had used a decade earlier, but managed no squirrels or squirrel potpie this time. We trolled for pickerel in the evening, again catching a beard of weeds instead of fish, and each evening toured the lake in the *Mitzi*. Jack, on the crest of three cocktails, entertained us all before and during each night's dinner with tales of his, Boyce's, and my mother's childhood and the pranks they had played on Grandfather. The weekend took place not long before I was to be married. My wife says it was her final test before being accepted into mystical union with an Adirondack-crazed nut.

For the full weekend I too was in thrall to nostalgia, but of a different sort. In the large coat closet off the living room, hanging from a hook on the door, was Grandfather's cane, just where he would have put it on returning from a conference with George out in the woodland park. On a shelf lay the Panama hat from which he used to drape a handkerchief, Legionnaire style, during the bug season. The domino set still sat in a drawer of his desk by the picture window, and draped over the back of one of the wicker sofas was the same steamer rug he used to throw over his legs on chilly late-August evenings. The guideboat and canoe were still in the boathouse, but the tin boat, in all its pristine crudeness, had either been sold or disposed of. As for the kitchen, the coal stove, Julia's implacable enemy, had been replaced by an efficient modern gas range, but in the pantry was the same old telephone, nearly as venerable as Alexander Graham Bell's original. In the silence of memory Julia's and Grandfather's voices, raised in long-resolved confrontation, were almost audible.

The visit ended with a flourish that recalled all the dear, dead days of the early 1930s. Sunday afternoon the Delco plant broke down, so that evening we huddled over dinner by candlelight and were all in bed by nine. In the middle of the night a violent thunderstorm passed over, its high winds toppling a large tree that blocked the road as we all tried to leave Monday morning. George, of course, cleared it away with an ax in no time. The combined inconvenience of a blocked road and no electricity convinced my father once again that the Adirondacks were fit only for blackflies. If a yacht can be defined as a hole in the water, surrounded by wood, into which one pours money, to my father a camp in the Adirondacks was no better. It was a Ponzi scheme, seducing the rich into thinking that to lead a simple life all they had to do was throw money at it.

CHAPTER ELEVEN

AFTER WORLD WAR II Woodwil was sold to the family of an executive prominent in the steel industry. With the benefit of new money, the camp rose like a phoenix from the travails of tenants and the war. Grandfather had made do with only eight double bedrooms, a primitive power plant, and a boathouse with two slips. But with five children, wads of cash, and a hearty appetite for the good things in life, the new owners set about doubling the size of the guidehouse so that now it can house sixteen people in eight double bedrooms. To the main lodge they added a master suite for Mom and Pop, and above the boathouse they built a second-floor playroom for Ping-Pong, billiards, mahjongg, Parcheesi, and what-have-you. Additional slips and dock space were added to one side of the boathouse to accommodate the various hydroplanes, jet skis, and other watercraft essential to dispel the boredom of an Adirondack vacation. A hundred yards down the road a splendid *en-tout-cas* tennis court, with a pleasant small lean-to for spectators, was hewn out of the forest. Finally, an underwater cable was laid to bring in honest-to-God electric power.

Certain features of the camp have remained unchanged. For example, the wicker furniture in the living room has been kept intact, with only new cushions and a lick of paint, as though Grandfather had struck the ultimate in Adirondack decor. The moose and deer heads, stuffed birds and fishes, have all retained their places on the

walls and newel posts, on the theory that they had been bagged by
gentlemanly Adirondack hunters, not bought like cordwood at secondhand stores. Grandfather's magnificent trusses and rustic fram-
ing over the broad verandah, once riddled with rot and decay, have
been restored to their former glory at no end of expense. Indeed, even
the "summer house," a charming little gazebo straddling the
wooden walk down to the boathouse, has been rebuilt log by log.
Thus, Woodwil once again has assumed the mantle of a Great Camp,
taking second place to no other establishment on Upper Saranac.
Perhaps Grandfather might have approved of Woodwil in its new
incarnation.

In a happy quirk of fortune the new owners bought only ten of
Grandfather's fifty acres, although my father, I am sure, would have
gladly sold them the remaining forty for spare change. This sale left
my cousin, John Robertson IV, and me as heirs presumptive to the
land. Missing hardly a beat, we set about building on my cousin's
property a serviceable small camp that over the years has become,
with the accretion of outbuildings and bunkhouses, electricity and
other amenities, a modest but comfortable family retreat.

But sharing houses, like guests overstaying their welcome, is at
best an accommodation to necessity. At the first blush of moderate
prosperity, my wife and I built our own camp some twenty-five years
ago. In conscious violation of most of the criteria of authentic
Adirondack architecture, our house has none of the fusty gloom or
contrived rusticity that gave Woodwil its inimitable, albeit handsome, character. Designed by William Shellman, a dear friend and
professor of architecture at Princeton University, the house has a
contemporary, Scandinavian look, with twenty feet of glass across
the front, vertical gray wood siding, and a twenty-by-thirty-foot deck
overlooking the lake. Inside are three tiny bedrooms, a pleasant living room, and a kitchen that also serves as a dining room.

The one concession to nostalgia (and that solely by coincidence because it was the architect's idea) is that two of the bedrooms, as at Woodwil, open onto a long balcony above the living room. In a gesture to rusticity we do not have and do not want electricity. We live off bottled propane gas that provides refrigeration and lights for the evening. Mounted on the living-room wall above the expanse of glass is our lone obeisance to Adirondack tradition, a deer head our second son bought as a gift lest we grow insolent in defying the sacred rites of the region.

Our house, along with my cousin's a short distance away, is located on the north shore of Grandfather's peninsula, on one of the lots he so hopefully laid out as building sites for other retired southern gentlemen. Both houses look out across the broad bay to where the Saranac Inn once stood. Just to the west of us is the high rock cliff where George Donaldson and his crew, in clearing the woodland park, used to build their huge brush fires each summer. Before us lies tiny Goose Island, which in our children's and in turn our grandchildren's day was a favorite camping site, and now is a challenge to a swimmer's endurance.

In time we added, for extra sleeping space, a small cabin that we built with our own hands—that is, the three boys and I—on a bluff just above the main house. There's also a genuine log cabin, constructed with trees cut right on the property. If you're not bothered by the occasional spider or whiskered beetle, it will give you the illusion of pioneer life. Finally, in a spendthrift gesture, we built some distance away a charming small A-frame with kitchen and bath intended as a retreat for my wife and me from the disturbances of children and grandchildren. We seldom use it.

The camp has no name; it is anonymous, just as I like to think all the forest surrounding us is. We are fortunate in that our place is located on perhaps the only acres of Grandfather's fifty that were not lumbered in Jack's madcap scheme. Everywhere there are tall pines and hemlocks a hundred years old and more. Several years ago, in clearing to let more light reach the A-frame, I was pointing out trees to be felled when the man doing the job indicated a huge yellow birch two or more feet in diameter.

"And is this one to go?" he asked.

"No," I answered, "I think we'll keep that one."

"A good thing," he said, " 'cause if you asked me, I wouldn't take it down. That tree's got to be at least two hundred years old, and there aren't many more like it around."

ASIDE FROM THE COMFORTS of life and our pleasure in the Nordic elegance of our small place, the greatest joy of the camp is its isolation and quiet. We are two and a half miles down Grandfather's private road, and our nearest neighbor—five families now share the point—is nearly a quarter mile away. Even then, a steep bluff shields us from all but the loudest noise. At night the nearest light lies at least two miles away across the water. It is a private world, the only intruders occasional fishermen who come for largemouth bass in the deep water by the rock cliffs and fallen trees that ring our small bay. Our seclusion is such that bathing suits are forbidden. In the evening, out on the deck, the silence is so deep that the splash of a fish surfacing for flies seems louder than voices heard through the living-room screens.

Here the serious business of life consists of pumping water to the large tank that supplies the house, trimming the kerosene lamps, swimming, and occasionally fishing or sailing our small boat. On summer evenings the wind usually drops at about six, and by seven Upper Saranac Lake is a sheen of dully glistening water. As dusk gathers, with the last blaze of sunset outlining the forest, the series of headlands beyond our bay look like the dark humps of fanciful, browsing animals nosing out into the water. Lights from faraway houses cast tiny arrows of brilliance on the flat black surface of the lake, and in an hour or so the sky will be a panoply of stars. But this moment of fading light is my favorite hour, as it was Grandfather's— "old father, old artificer" that he was.